GREAT THINKERS

Get closer to some of the world's most astute minds, past and present, as we celebrate those who challenge and inspire us.

AC GRAYLING & ROWAN WILLIAMS

Wednesday 11 May

With *The Good Book*, AC Grayling has created a secular bible, which he discusses with Rowan Williams, Archbishop of Canterbury.

FRANCIS FUKUYAMA

Monday 16 May

One of the most dynamic and provocative thinkers of modern times discusses his new work, *The Origins of Political Order*, and takes questions from the audience.

PAUL THEROUX

Tuesday 24 May

Hear one of the world's great travel writers talk about his latest book, *The Tao of Travel*.

JOHN BERGER

Wednesday 25 May

John Berger discusses *Bento's Sketchbook* – a clear-sighted meditation on how we perceive and seek to explain the world around us.

BETTANY HUGHES

Thursday 2 June

Bettany Hughes discusses Socrates – a cornerstone of Western thought who she argues was the world's first documented ideological martyr.

ALSO THIS SPRING

TONY BENN

Monday 23 May

One of our greatest political figures looks back on a long history of English radicalism and explores what radicalism can mean today.

ORANGE PRIZE SHORTLIST READINGS

Monday 6 June

Hear the writers shortlisted for this year's prize read from their work.

Photo: John Berger

SOUTHBANK CENTRE

Supported by
ARTS COUNCIL
ENGLAND

TICKETS: 0844 847 9910
SOUTHBANKCENTRE.CO.UK

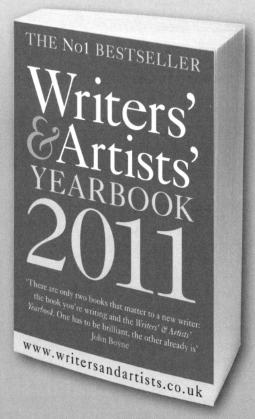

CONTENTS

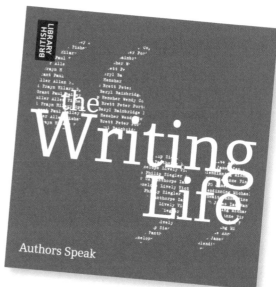

GRANTA

AFTERMATH

Rachel Cusk

Recently my husband and I separated, and over the course of a few weeks the life that we'd made broke apart, like a jigsaw dismantled into a heap of broken-edged pieces.

Sometimes the matrix of a jigsaw is undetectable in the assembled picture; there are champion jigsaw-makers who pride themselves on such things, but mostly you can tell. The light falls on the surface indentations – it's only from far away that the image seems complete. My younger daughter likes doing jigsaws. The older one does not: she builds card houses in whose environs everyone must remain silent and still. I see in these activities differing attempts to exert control, but I am struck too by the proof they provide that there is more than one way of being patient, and that intolerance can take many forms. My daughters take these variations in temperament a little too seriously. Each resents the opposing tendency in the other; in fact, I would almost say that they pursue their separate activities as a form of argument. An argument is only an emergency of self-definition, after all. And I've wondered from time to time whether it is one of the pitfalls of modern family life, with its relentless jollity, its entirely unfounded optimism, its reliance not on God or economics but on the principle of love, that it fails to recognize – and to take precautions against – the human need for war.

'The new reality' was a phrase that kept coming up in those early weeks: people used it to describe my situation, as though it might represent a kind of progress. But it was in fact a regression: the gears of life had gone into reverse. All at once we were moving not forwards but backwards, back into chaos, into history and pre-history, back to the beginnings of things and then further back to the time before those things began. A plate falls to the floor: the new reality is that it is broken. I had to get used to the new reality. My two young daughters had to get used to the new reality. But the new reality, as far as I could see, was only something broken. It had been created and for years it had served its purpose, but in pieces – unless they could be glued back together – it was good for nothing at all.

My husband believed that I had treated him monstrously. This belief of his couldn't be shaken: his whole world depended on it. It was his story, and lately I have come to hate stories. If someone were to ask me what disaster this was that had befallen my life, I might ask if they wanted the story or the truth. I might say, by way of explanation, that an important vow of obedience had been broken. I might explain that when I write a novel wrong, eventually it breaks down and stops and won't be written any more, and I have to go back and look for the flaws in its design. The problem usually lies in the relationship between the story and the truth. The story has to obey the truth, to represent it, like clothes represent the body. The closer the cut, the more pleasing the effect. Unclothed, truth can be vulnerable, ungainly, shocking. Overdressed, it becomes a lie. For me, life's difficulty has generally lain in the attempt to reconcile these two, like the child of divorce tries to reconcile its parents. My own children do that, forcing my husband's hand into mine when we're all together. They're trying to make the story true again, or to make the truth untrue. I'm happy enough to hold his hand but my husband doesn't like it. It's bad form – and form is important in stories. Everything that was formless in our life together now belongs to me. So it doesn't trouble me, doesn't bother me to hold his hand. There should probably be more hand-holding in the world generally. This was the kind of thing I had started to think.

After a while, time stopped going backwards. Even so, we had regressed quite a long way. In those few weeks, we had undone everything that led to the moment of our separation; we had undone history itself. There was nothing left to be dismantled, except the children, and that would require the intervention of science. But we were before science: we had gone back to something like seventh-century Britain, before the advent of nationhood. England was in those days a country of compartments: I remember, at school, looking at a map of the early medieval heptarchy and feeling a kind of consternation at its diffusity, its lack of centralized power, its absence of king and capital city and institution. Instead, there were merely regions whose names – Mercia, Wessex – fell effeminately on the ears, and whose ceaseless squabblings and small, laborious losses and gains seemed to lack a driving, unifying force that I might, had I cared to think about it, have identified as masculine.

Our history teacher, Mrs Lewis, was a woman of size and grace, a type of elephant-ballerina in whom the principles of bulk and femininity fought a war of escalation. The early medieval was her period: she had studied at Oxford, and now here she was in the classroom of our mediocre Catholic girls' school, encased in a succession of beige tailored outfits with coordinating heels from which it seemed her mighty pink form might one day startlingly emerge, like a statue from its dust sheets. The other thing we knew about her, from her name, was that she was married. But how these different aspects of Mrs Lewis connected we had no idea. She gave great consideration to Offa of Mercia, in whose vision of a unified England the first thrust of male ambition can be detected, and whose massive earthwork, Offa's Dyke, still stands as a reminder that division is also an aspect of unification, that one way of defining what you are is to define what you are not. And indeed historians have never been able to agree on the question of whether the dyke was built to repel the Welsh or merely to mark the boundary. Mrs Lewis took an ambivalent attitude to Offa's power: this was the road to civilization, sure enough, but its cost was a loss of diversity, of the quiet kind of flourishing that goes on where things are not being built and goals driven towards. She herself relished the early Saxon world, in which concepts of power had not yet been reconfigured; for in a way the Dark Ages were themselves a version of 'the new reality', the broken pieces of the biggest plate of all, the Roman Empire. Some called it darkness, the aftermath of that megalomaniacal all-conquering unity, but not Mrs Lewis. She liked it, liked the untenanted wastes, liked the monasteries where creativity was quietly nurtured, liked the mystics and the visionaries, the early religious writings, liked the women who accrued stature in those formless inchoate centuries, liked the grass roots – the personal level on which issues of justice and belief had now to be resolved, in the absence of that great administrator civilization.

The point was that this darkness – call it what you will – this darkness and disorganization were not mere negation, mere absence. They were both aftermath and prelude. The etymology of the word 'aftermath' is 'second mowing': a second crop of grass that is sown and reaped after the harvest is in. Civilization, order, meaning, belief: these were not sunlit peaks to be reached by a steady climb. They were built and then they fell, were built and fell again or were destroyed. The darkness, the disorganization that succeeded them had their own existence, their own integrity; were betrothed to civilization, as sleep is betrothed to activity. In the life of compartments lies the possibility of unity, just as unity contains the prospect of atomization. Better, in Mrs Lewis's view, to live the compartmentalized, disorganized life and feel the dark stirrings of creativity than to dwell in civilized unity, racked by the impulse to destroy.

In the mornings I take my daughters to school and mid-afternoon I pick them up again. I tidy their rooms and do laundry and cook. We spend the evenings mostly alone; I do their homework with them and feed them and put them to bed. Every few days they go to their father's and then the house is empty. At first these interludes were difficult to bear. Now they have a kind of neutrality about them, something firm but blank, something faintly accusatory despite the blankness. It is as though these solitary hours, in which for the first time in many years nothing is expected or required of me, are my spoils of war, are what I have received in exchange for all this conflict. I live them one after another. I swallow them down like hospital food. In this way I am kept alive. I live them one after another, processing my sickness, surviving.

Call yourself a feminist, my husband would say to me, disgustedly, in the raw bitter weeks after we separated. He believed he had taken the part of woman in our marriage, and seemed to expect me to defend him against myself, the male oppressor. He felt it was womanly to shop and cook, to collect the children from school. Yet it was when I myself did those things that I often felt most unsexed. My own mother had not seemed beautiful to me in the exercise of her maternal duties; likewise they seemed to threaten, not enhance, her womanliness. In those days we lived in a village in the flat Suffolk countryside; she seemed to spend a great deal of time on the telephone. The sound of her voice talking as though to itself was somehow maddening. Her phrases sounded scripted, her laughter artificial. I suspected her of using a special voice, like an actress. This superficial woman was an impostor – my mother was someone I could never see or hear that clearly. Instead, I seemed to share her point of view, seemed to dwell within her boredom or pleasure or irritation. Her persona was like a second, phantasmagoric house that existed inside our actual house: it was where I lived, unseeing. How could I know what my mother was? How could I see her? For her attention felt like the glance of some inner eye that never looked at me straight, that took its knowledge from my own private knowledge of myself.

It was only when she was with other people that, as a child, I was able to notice her objectively. Sometimes she would have a female friend round to lunch and then all at once there it would be, my mother's face. Suddenly I could see her, could compare her to this other woman and find her better or worse, could see her being liked or envied or provoked, could know her particular habits and her atmosphere, which were not those of this other. At such times her persona, my dwelling place, was inaccessible to me, darkened, like an empty house. If I knocked at the door I was curtly – sometimes roughly – dispatched. Her body, usually so extensive, so carelessly ubiquitous, seemed to have been packed up and put away. And she too was locked out, relieved for a while of the business of being herself. Instead she was performing; she was pure story, told badly or well.

Her friends were generally mothers too, women whose geography I recognized, the sense of an enigma that lay all around their masks of make-up and talk like open countryside around a city. You could never get out into that countryside but you knew it was there. She did have one friend, Jane, who was different from the others. At the time I didn't understand why, but now I do: Jane didn't have children. She was a large woman, a wit, though her face was sad. You could walk around in the sadness of her mouth and eyes; it was open to everyone. She came once when my mother had made a chocolate cake, for which she tried to give Jane the recipe. Jane said, 'If I made that cake I'd just eat the whole thing in one sitting.' I had never heard of a woman eating a whole cake. It struck me as a tremendous feat, like weightlifting. But I could tell that my mother didn't like this remark. In some obscure sense Jane had given the game away. Not knowing any better, she had opened up a chink in the tall wall of womanhood, and given me a rare glimpse of what was on the other side.

Of certain parts of life there can be no foreknowledge – war, for instance. The soldier going to war for the first time does not know how he will behave when confronted by an armed enemy. He does not know this part of himself. Is he killer or coward? When confronted he will respond, yet he doesn't know in advance what his response will be.

My husband said that he wanted half of everything, including the children. No, I said. What do you mean no, he said. This was on the telephone. I looked out of the window at the garden, a rectangle among other urban rectangles, the boundaries prowled by cats. Lately our garden had become overgrown. The beds were drowning in weeds. The grass was long, like hair. But no matter how disorderly it became the grid would be undisturbed: the other rectangles would hold their shape regardless.

You can't divide people in half, I said.

They should be with me half the time, he said.

They're my children, I said. They belong to me.

In Greek drama, to traduce biological human roles is to court the change that is death, the death that is change. The vengeful mother, the selfish father, the perverted family, the murderous child – these are the bloody roads to democracy, to justice. The children belong to me: once I would have criticized such a sentiment severely. Where had this heresy gestated? If it was part of me, where had it lived for all those years, in our egalitarian household? Where had it hidden itself? My mother liked to talk about the early English Catholics forced to live and worship in secrecy, sleeping in cupboards or underneath the floorboards. To her it seemed extraordinary that the true beliefs should have to hide themselves. Was this, in fact, a persecuted truth, and our own way of life the heresy?

I said it again: I couldn't help myself. I said it to my friend Eleanor; that the children belonged to me. Eleanor has a job, is often away for weeks at a time; her husband takes over when she's not there, putting their children to bed, handing them over to the nanny in the morning. Eleanor pursed her mouth and disapprovingly shook her head a little. Children belong just as much to their fathers as to their mothers, she said. I said to my friend Anna, who has no job and four children, the children belong to me. Anna's husband works long hours. She manages the children largely alone, as I now do. Yes, she says, they're your children. You're the one they need. They should be your number-one priority.

It has existed in a kind of banishment, my flesh history with my daughters. Have I been, as a mother, denied? The long pilgrimage of pregnancy with its wonders and abasements, the apotheosis of childbirth, the sacking and slow rebuilding of every last corner of my private world that motherhood has entailed – all unmentioned, wilfully or casually forgotten as time has passed, the Dark Ages on which I now feel the civilization of our family has been built. And I was part of that pact of silence, in a way: it was a condition of the treaty that gave me my equality, that I would not invoke the primitivism of the mother, her innate superiority, that voodoo in the face of which the mechanism of equal rights breaks down. My own mother once wept at the supper table, wildly accusing us of never having thanked her for giving birth to us. And we joked about it later, cruel teenaged sophisticates. We felt uneasy, and rightly so: we had been unjustly blamed. Wasn't it my father who should have thanked her, for giving form and substance, continuance, to himself? Instead, his own contribution, his work, ran parallel to hers: it was she who had to be grateful to him, superficially at least. For years he had gone to the office and come back again, regular as a Swiss train, as authorized as she was illicit. The rationality of this behaviour was what irrationalized hers, for her womanhood was all imposition and cause, all profligacy, a kind of problem to which his work was the solution. How could she expect gratitude for what no one seemed to think of as a gift? Through her we all of us served the cause of life: she was the exacting representative of our dumb master, nature. She gave, as nature gives, but we were not going to survive in nature on mere gratitude. We had to tame, to cultivate her gifts; and, increasingly, we ourselves took all the credit for the results. We were in league with civilization.

Like God, my father expressed himself through absence; it was easier, perhaps, to be grateful to someone who wasn't there. He too seemed to obey the call of civilization, to recognize it when it spoke. As rational beings we allied ourselves with him, against the paganism of my mother, her orgies of emotion, her gaze forever dwelling on what was done and past or on the relieving blankness of what was yet to come. These qualities seemed to be without origin: they belonged neither to motherhood nor to herself, but to some eternal fact that arose out of the conjunction of the two. I knew, of course, that once upon a time she had had her own reality, had lived, as it were, in real time. In the wedding photograph that stood on the mantelpiece, her former slenderness was always arresting. There she stood in white, the sacrificial victim: a narrow-waisted smiling beauty, as compact as a seed. The key, the genius of it all, seemed to lie in how little of her there was. In the finely graven lines of her beauty, our whole sprawling future was encrypted. That beauty was gone now, all used up, like the oil that is sucked out of the earth for the purpose of combustion. The world has grown bloated, disorganized, wasteful on oil. Sometimes

– looking at that photograph – my family seemed like the bloated product of my mother's beauty.

But for me the notion of a woman's beauty had somewhere in the course of things become theoretical, like the immigrant's notion of home. And in the generational transition between my mother and myself, a migration of sorts had indeed occurred. My mother may have been my place of birth, but my adopted nationality was my father's. She had aspired to marriage and motherhood, to being desired and possessed by a man in a way that would legitimize her. I myself was the fruit of those aspirations but somehow, in the evolution from her to me, it had become my business to legitimize myself. Yet my father's aspirations – to succeed, to win, to provide – did not quite fit me either: they were like a suit of clothes made for someone else, but they were what was available. So I wore them and felt a little uncomfortable, a little unsexed, but clothed all the same. Both my parents encouraged this form of cross-dressing, my mother as liable as my father to be displeased by a bad school report or a mediocre grade, despite the fact that she herself had no A levels. I got into Oxford, my sister to Cambridge, egged on by them both, immigrants to the new country of sexual equality who hoped to achieve assimilation through the second generation.

One is formed by what one's parents say and do; and one is formed by what one's parents are. But what happens when what they say and what they are don't match? My father, a man, advanced male values to us, his daughters. And my mother, a woman, did the same. So it was my mother who didn't match, who didn't make sense. We belong as much to our moment in history as to our parents; I suppose it would have been reprehensible, in Britain in the late twentieth century, for her to have told us not to worry about our maths, that the important thing was to find a nice husband to support us. Yet her own mother had probably told her precisely that. There was nothing, as a woman, she could bequeath us; nothing to pass on from mother to daughter but these adulterated male values. And of that forsaken homeland, beauty, which now lay so despoiled – as the countryside around our Suffolk home was in the years of my growing up despoiled; disfigured by new roads and houses that it pained my oversensitive eyes to look at – of beauty, a woman's beauty, of the place I had come from, I knew nothing at all. I didn't know its manners or its customs. I didn't speak its language. In that world of femininity where I had the right to claim citizenship, I was an alien.

Call yourself a feminist, my husband says. And perhaps one of these days I'll say to him, yes, you're right. I shouldn't call myself a feminist. You're right. I'm so terribly sorry.

And in a way, I'll mean it. What is a feminist, anyway? What does it mean, to call yourself one? There are men who call themselves feminists. There are women who are anti-feminist. A feminist man is a bit like a vegetarian: it's the humanitarian principle he's defending, I suppose. Sometimes feminism seems to involve so much criticism of female modes of being that you could be forgiven for thinking that a feminist is a woman who hates women, hates them for being such saps. Then again, the feminist is supposed to hate men. She scorns the physical and emotional servitude they exact. She calls them *the enemy.*

In any case, she wouldn't be found haunting the scene of the crime, as it were; loitering in the kitchen, in the maternity ward, at the school gate. She knows that her womanhood is a fraud, manufactured by others for their own convenience; she knows that women are not born but made. So she stays away from it – the kitchen, the maternity ward – like the alcoholic stays away from the bottle. Some alcoholics have a fantasy of modest social drinking: they just haven't been through enough cycles of failure yet. The woman who thinks she can *choose* femininity, can toy with it like the social drinker toys with wine – well, she's asking for it, asking to be undone, devoured, asking to spend her life perpetrating a new fraud, manufacturing a new fake identity, only this time it's her equality that's fake. Either she's doing twice as much as she did before, or she sacrifices her equality and does less than she should. She's two women, or she's half a woman.

And either way she'll have to say, because she chose it, that she's enjoying herself.

So I suppose a feminist wouldn't get married. She wouldn't have a joint bank account or a house in joint names. She might not have children either, girl children whose surname is not their mother's but their father's, so that when she travels abroad with them they have to swear to the man at passport control that she *is* their mother. No, I shouldn't have called myself a feminist, because what I said didn't match with what I was: just like my mother, only the other way round.

What I lived as feminism were in fact the male values my parents, among others, well-meaningly bequeathed me – the cross-dressing values of my father, and the anti-feminine values of my mother. So I am not a feminist. I am a self-hating transvestite.

Like many women I know, I have never been supported financially by a man. This is anecdotal information – women have a weakness for that. And perhaps a feminist is someone who possesses this personalizing trait to a larger-than-average degree: she is an autobiographer, an artist of the self. She acts as an interface between private and public, just as women always have, except that the feminist does it in reverse. She does not propitiate: she objects. She's a woman turned inside out.

If you live long enough, the anecdotal becomes the statistical in any case. You emerge with your cohorts out of the jungle of middle life, each possessing your own private knowledge of courage or cowardice, and do a quick headcount, an inventory of missing limbs. I know women with four children and women with no children, divorced women and married women, successful and compromised women, apologetic, ambitious and contented women, women who are unfulfilled or accepting, selfless and frustrated women. And some of them, it is true, are not financially dependent on men. What can I say about the ones that are? That they're usually full-time mothers. And that they live more through their children. That's how it seems to me. The child goes through the full-time mother like a dye through water: there is no part of her that remains uncoloured. The child's triumphs and losses are her triumphs and losses. The child's beauty is her beauty, as is the child's unacceptability. And because management of the child is her job, her own management of the world is conducted through it. Her subjectivity has more than one source, and only a single outlet. This can result in extreme competence: some of my friends claim to find such women frightening or threatening. These friends are generally women who sustain more than one identity out of a single self, and hence perhaps fear accusations of extreme incompetence. Their power is diffuse: they never feel it collected in one place, and as a result they don't know how much of it there is, whether they have less or more power than that curiously titled creature, the stay-at-home mum, or indeed than their male colleagues at work who must, I suppose, share at least some of their feelings of scatteration.

A few of these working-mother friends of mine have taken the occasional domestic furlough, usually in the early years of parenthood. Like wanted criminals finally run to ground, they surrender with their hands up: yes, it was all too much, too unworkable, the running hither and thither, the guilt, the pressure at work, the pressure at home, the question of why – if you were never going to see them – you went to the trouble of having children in the first place. So they decide to stay at home for a year or two and even things up a bit, like the cake mixture the recipe tells you to divide between two tins, of which there always seems to be more in one than the other. Their husbands also work, live in the same houses and parent the same children, yet don't seem to experience quite the same measure of conflict. In fact, sometimes they actually look like they're better at being working parents than women are – insufferable male superiority!

But a man commits no particular heresy against his sex by being a good father, and working is part of what a good father does. The working mother, on the other hand, is traducing her role in the founding myths of civilization on a daily basis – no wonder she's a little harassed. She's trying to defy her own deep-seated relationship with gravity. I read somewhere that a space station is always slowly falling back to Earth, and that every few months or so a rocket has to be sent to push it back out again. In rather the same way, a woman is forever dragged at by an imperceptible force of biological conformism: her life is relentlessly iterative; it requires energy to keep her in orbit. Year after year she'll do it, but if one year the rocket doesn't come then down she'll go.

The stay-at-home mum often describes herself as lucky: that's her pitch, her line, should anyone – a working mother, for instance – care to enquire. We're so lucky that James's salary means I don't have to work, she'll say, as though she took a huge punt on a single horse and found that she'd backed a winner. You don't catch a man saying he feels lucky to be able to go to the office every day. Yet the stay-at-home mum often calls it a privilege, to be 'allowed' to do her traditional and entirely unexceptional domestic work. It's a defensive statement, of course – she doesn't want to be thought of as lazy or unambitious – and like much defensiveness it (barely) conceals a core of aggression. Yet presumably she is elated when her daughter comes top in the maths test, gets a place at Cambridge, becomes a nuclear physicist. Does she wish it for her daughter, that privilege, the time-immemorial life at home with children? Or does she think this is a riddle that someone in the future will somehow just solve, like scientists inventing the cure for cancer?

I remember, when my own children were born, when I first held them and fed them and talked to them, feeling a great awareness of this new, foreign aspect of myself that was in me and yet did not seem to be of me. It was as though I had suddenly acquired the ability to speak Russian: what I could do – this women's work – had so much form of its own, yet I didn't know where my knowledge of it had come from. In some ways I wanted to claim the knowledge as mine, as innate, but to do that seemed to involve a strange kind of dishonesty, a pretending. And yet, how could I pretend to be what I already was? I felt inhabited by a second self, a twin whose jest it was – in the way of twins – to appear to be me while doing things that were alien to my own character. Yet this twin was not apparently malign: she was just asking for a degree of freedom, a temporary release from the strict protocol of identity. She wanted to act as a woman, a generic woman, but character is not generic. It is entirely and utterly specific. To act as a mother, I had to suspend my own character, which had evolved on a diet of male values. And my habitat, my environment, had evolved that way too. An adaptation would be required. But who was going to do the adapting? I was aware, in those early days, that my behaviour was strange to the people who knew me well. It was as though I had been brainwashed, taken over by a cult religion. I had gone away – I couldn't be reached on the usual number. And yet this cult, motherhood, was not a place where I could actually live. It reflected nothing about me: its literature and practices, its values, its codes of conduct, its aesthetic were not mine. It was generic too: like any cult, it demanded a complete surrender of identity to belong to it. So for a while I didn't belong anywhere. As the mother of young children I was homeless, drifting, itinerant. And I felt an inadmissible pity for myself and for my daughters in those years. It seemed almost catastrophic to me, the disenchantment of this contact with womanhood. Like the adopted child who finally locates its parents only to discover that they are loveless strangers, my inability to find a home as a mother impressed me as something not about the world but about my own unwantedness. I seemed, as a woman, to be extraneous.

And so I did two things: I reverted to my old male-inflected identity; and I conscripted my husband into care of the children. He was to take the part of that twin, femininity. He was to offer her a body of her own to shelter in, for she didn't seem able to find peace in me. My notion was that we would live together as two hybrids, each of us half male and half female. That was equality, was it not? He gave up his law job, and I gave up the exclusivity of my primitive maternal right over the children. These were our preparatory sacrifices to the new gods, whose future protection we hoped to live under. Ten years later, sitting in a solicitor's office on a noisy main road in north London, my maternalism did indeed seem primitive to me, almost barbaric. The children belong to me – this was not the kind of rudimentary phrase-making I generally went in for. Yet it was the only thought in my head, there in the chrome-and-glass office, with the petite solicitor in tailored black sitting opposite. I was thin and gaunt with distress, yet in her presence I felt enormous, rough-hewn, a maternal rock encrusted with ancient ugly emotion. She told me I had no rights of any kind. The law in these cases didn't operate on the basis of rights. What mattered was the precedent, and the precedent could be as unprecedented as you liked. So there was no primitive reality after all, it seemed. There was no such thing as a mother, a father. There was only civilization. She told me I was obliged to support my husband financially, possibly forever. But he's a qualified lawyer, I said. And I'm just a writer. What I meant was, he's a man. And I'm just a woman. The old voodoo still banging its drum, there in the heart of marital darkness. The solicitor raised her slender eyebrows, gave me a bitter little smile. Well, then he knew exactly what he was doing, she said.

Summer came, clanging days of glaring sunshine in the seaside town where I live, the gulls screaming in the early dawn, a glittering agitation everywhere, the water a vista of smashed light. I could no longer sleep; my consciousness filled up with the lumber of dreams, of broken-edged sections of the past heaving and stirring in the undertow. At the school gate, collecting my daughters, the other women looked somehow quaint to me, as people look when seen across a distance. I saw them as though from the annihilated emptiness of the ocean, people inhabiting land, inhabiting a construction. They had not destroyed their homes. Why had I destroyed my home? Visiting my sister, I sat in her kitchen while she folded laundry. I watched her fold her husband's shirts, his trousers. It shocked me to see these male garments, to see her touching them. She seemed to be touching something forbidden. Her right to handle these forbidden items overwhelmed me.

You know the law, my husband said over the phone. He was referring to my obligation to give him money.

I know what's right, I said.

Call yourself a feminist, he said.

What I need is a wife, jokes the stressed-out feminist career woman, and everyone laughs. The joke is that the feminist's pursuit of male values has led her to the threshold of female exploitation. This is irony. Get it? The feminist scorns that silly complicit creature, the housewife. Her first feminist act may have been to try to liberate her own housewife mother, and discover that rescue was neither wanted nor required. I hated my mother's unwaged status, her servitude, her domesticity, undoubtedly more than she herself did, for she never said she disliked them at all. Yet I stood accused of recreating exactly those conditions in my own adult life. I had hated my husband's unwaged domesticity just as much as I had hated my mother's; and he, like her, had claimed to be contented with his lot. Why had I hated it so? Because it represented dependence. But there was more to it than that, for it might be said that dependence is an agreement between two people. My father depended on my mother too: he couldn't cook a meal, or look after children from the office. They were two halves that made up a whole. What, morally speaking, is half a person? Yet the two halves were not the same: in a sense my parents were a single compartmentalized human being. My father's half was very different from my mother's, but despite the difference neither half made any sense on its own. So it was in the difference that the problem lay.

My notion of half was more like the earthworm's: you cut it in two but each half remains an earthworm, wriggling and fending for itself. I earned the money in our household, did my share of the cooking and cleaning, paid someone to look after the children while I worked, picked them up from school once they were older. And my husband helped. It was his phrase, and still is: he helped me. I was the compartmentalized modern woman, the woman having it all, and he helped me to be it, to have it. But I didn't want help: I wanted equality. In fact, this idea of help began to annoy me. Why couldn't we be the same? Why couldn't he be compartmentalized too? And why, exactly, was it helpful for a man to look after his own children, or cook the food that he himself would eat? Helpful is what a good child is to its mother. A helpful person is someone who performs duties outside their own sphere of responsibility, out of the kindness of their heart. Help is dangerous because it exists outside the human economy: the only payment for help is gratitude. And did I not have something of the same gratuitous tone where my wage-earning was concerned? Did I not think there was something awfully helpful about me, a woman, supporting my own family?

And so I felt, beneath the reconfigured surface of things, the tension of the old orthodoxies. We were a man and a woman who in our struggle for equality had simply changed clothes. We were two transvestites, a transvestite couple – well, why not? Except that I did both things, was both man and woman, while my husband – meaning well – only did one. Once, a female friend confessed to me that she admired our life but couldn't have lived it herself. She admitted the reason – that she would no longer respect her husband if he became a wife. We were, then, admirable – me for not needing a man, and him for being willing not to be one. But the admiration interested me. What, precisely, was being admired? And how could what was admirable entail the loss of respect?

Sometimes my awareness of my own competence alarmed me. How would I remain attached to the world if not by need? I didn't appear to need anyone: I could do it all myself. I could do everything. I was both halves: did that mean I was whole? In a sense I was living at the high point of feminist possibility: there was no blueprint beyond 'having it all'. The richness of that phrase, its suggestion of an unabashed splendour, was apposite. To have both motherhood and work was to have two lives instead of one, was a stunning refinement of historical female experience, and to the people who complained that having it all meant doing it all I would have said, yes, of course it does. You don't get 'all' for nothing. 'Having it all', like any form of success, requires hard work. It requires an adoption of the heroic mode of being. But the hero is solitary, individualistic, set apart from the human community. She is a wanderer, forever searching out the Holy Grail, forever questing, pursuing the goal that will provide the accurate reflection of her own abilities. The hero, being exceptional, is essentially alone.

So I was both man and woman, but over time the woman sickened, for her gratifications were fewer. I had to keep out of the way, keep out of the kitchen, keep a certain distance from my children, not only to define my husband's femininity but also to appease my own male values. The oldest trick in the sexist book is the female need for control of children. I perceived in the sentimentality and narcissism of motherhood a threat to the objectivity that as a writer I valued so highly. But it wasn't control of the children I was necessarily sickening for. It was something subtler – prestige, the prestige that is the mother's reward for the work of bearing her offspring. And that prestige was my husband's. I had given it to him or he had taken it – either way, it was what he got out of our arrangement. And the domestic work I did was in a sense at the service of that prestige, for it encompassed the menial, the trivial, the frankly boring, as though I were busily working behind the scenes to ensure the smooth running of the spectacle on-stage. I wasn't male after all – men didn't do drudgery. And I wasn't female either: I felt ugly, for the things that were mine – dirty laundry, VAT returns – were not pretty at all. In fact, there was nothing pretty that gave me back a reflection of myself. I went to Paris for two days with my husband, determined while I was there to have my hair cut in a French salon. Wasn't this what women did? Well, I wanted to be womanized; I wanted someone to restore to me my lost femininity. A male hairdresser cut off all my hair, giggling as he did it, amusing himself during a boring afternoon at the salon by giving a tired blank-faced mother of two something punky and *nouvelle vague*. Afterwards, I wandered in the Paris streets, anxiously catching my reflection in shop windows. Had a transformation occurred, or a defacement? I wasn't sure. My husband wasn't sure either. It seemed terrible that between us we couldn't establish the truth. It seemed terrible, in broad daylight, in those public anonymous streets, not to know.

Sometimes, in the bath, the children cry. Their nakedness, or the warm water, or the comfort of the old routine – something, anyway, dislodges their sticking-plaster emotions and shows the wound beneath. It is my belief that I gave them that wound, so now I must take all the blame. Another version of the heroic, where the hero and the villain are hard to tell apart.

I wounded them and in this way I learned truly to love them. Or rather, I admitted it, admitted this love, admitted how much of it there was. I externalized it; internalized, it had been an instrument of self-torture. But now it was out in the world, visible, practical. What is a loving mother? It is someone whose self-interest has been displaced into her actual children. Her children's suffering causes her more pain than her own: it is Mary at the foot of the cross. In church, at the Easter service, I used to be struck by the description of Mary's emotional state, for amid that drama of physical torment it was said that she felt as though a sword had been run through her heart. It interested me that such an image was applied to her feelings, an image that came to her from the cold hard outer world, from the physical plane of men. Somehow, in the transition from other to mother, the active becomes passive, the actual theoretical, the physical emotional, the objective subjective. The blow is softened: when my children cry a sword is run through my heart. Yet it is I who am also the cause of their crying. And for a while I am undone by this contradiction, by the difficulty of connecting the person who acted out of self-interest with the heartbroken mother who has succeeded her. It seems to be the fatal and final evolution of the compartmentalized woman, a kind of personality disorder, like schizophrenia.

Winter comes: the days are brief and pale, the sea retracted as though into unconsciousness. The coldly silvered water turns quietly on the shingle. There are long nights of stars and frost, and in the morning frozen puddles lie like little smashed mirrors in the road. We sleep many hours, like people recovering from an operation. Pain is so vivid, yet the stupor of recovery is such that pain's departure often goes unnoticed. You simply realize, one day, that it has gone, leaving a curious blank in the memory, a feeling of transitive mystery, as though the person who suffered is not – not quite – the same as the person who now walks around well. Another compartment has been created, this one for keeping odds and ends in, stray parts of experience, questions for which the answers were never found.

We rearrange the furniture to cover up the gaps. We economize, take in a lodger, get a fish tank. The fish twirl and pirouette eternally amid the fronds, regardless of what day it is. The children go to their father's and come back again. They no longer cry: they complain heartily about the inconvenience of the new arrangements. They have colour in their faces. A friend comes to stay and remarks on the sound of laughter in the house, like birdsong after the silence of winter. But it is winter still: we go to a Christmas carol service and I watch the other families. I watch mother and father and children. And I see it so clearly, as though I were looking in at them through a brightly lit window from the darkness outside; see the story in which they play their roles, their parts, with the whole world as a backdrop. We're not part of that story any more, my children and I. We belong more to the world, in all its risky disorder, its fragmentation, its freedom. The world is constantly evolving, while the family endeavours to stay the same. Updated, refurbished, modernized, but essentially the same. A house in the landscape, both shelter and prison.

We sing the carols, a band of three. I have sung these songs since my earliest recollection, sung them year after year: first as a tradition-loving child in the six-strong conventional family pew; later as a young woman who most ardently called herself a feminist; later still as a wife and mother in whose life these irreconcilable principles – the traditional and the radical, the story and the truth – had out of their hostility hatched a kind of cancer. Looking at the other families I feel our stigma, our loss of prestige: we are like a Gypsy caravan parked up among the houses, itinerant, temporary. I see that we have lost a degree of protection, of certainty. I see that I have exchanged one kind of prestige for another, one set of values for another, one scale for another. I see too that we are more open, more capable of receiving than we were; that should the world prove to be a generous and wondrous place, we will perceive its wonders.

I begin to notice, looking in through those imaginary brightly lit windows, that the people inside are looking out. I see the women, these wives and mothers, looking out. They seem happy enough, contented enough, capable enough: they are well dressed, attractive, standing with their men and their children. Yet they look around, their mouths moving. It is as though they are missing something or wondering about something. I remember it so well, what it was to be one of them. Sometimes one of these glances will pass over me and our eyes will briefly meet. And I realize she can't see me, this woman whose eyes have locked with mine. It isn't that she doesn't want to, or is trying not to. It's just that inside it's so bright and outside it's so dark, and so she can't see out, can't see anything at all. ■

Coronation

By and by, the balustrade.

We waited quietly for the Queen who wasn't there, whose car –

The moon of alabaster.

Light of men

that lay across her throat, a thwart scar.

Bitter, the heart's sweet thought of –

Nothing but

the gold abyss of God.

We waited, quietly, for.

The flying buttress of the sea, put by.

Because they have taken away my Lord, and I –

NOTE

l.2   Summer 1953: we waited in front of my great-aunt's house in New Cross, south London, to wave to the Queen as she was driven past in an open-topped car.

l.4   John 1:4

l.11   John 20:13

NO GRLS ALOD. INSEPT MOM.*

A.S. Byatt

*Notice attached to his bedroom door by my five-year-old grandson.

There are incidents in my life that I think of together – times when I was stopped suddenly short by blank, unexpected and obvious reminders of the disadvantages of my sex. The first was when I was a clever girl at a boarding school – perhaps fifteen years old – being taken out to tea by my father, a barrister, with another elegant lawyer who was his friend. We sat on upholstered chairs in a sunny drawing room in a grand hotel, and had tea from a silver teapot, and triangular sandwiches, and pretty sweet buns. I was asked to be mother and poured the tea.

I was shy and said little unless spoken to. My father's friend asked kindly what I was going to be when I grew up.

'An ambassador,' I said. I was very good at languages, I loved them.

'You mean, an ambassador's wife,' my father's friend corrected me, still kindly.

I was shocked. I said no, I meant an ambassador. I wanted to use my languages. I already had a horror of being defined as a wife.

'Women can't be ambassadors, I'm afraid,' he said still kindly, but finally. I had led a sequestered life in a mostly female world. I was dreadfully shocked. I rearranged my suddenly limited horizons in my head with some distress.

I do not have a naturally political temperament. I went to Cambridge in the fifties. I knew that women undergraduates weren't admitted to the union, but I didn't want to go there. There was so much else to do and I had never cared for formal debating. I didn't think clearly enough.

My moment of pure feminist rage came when I was a very young academic wife in Durham in the early sixties. Durham University in those days was modelled on Oxford and Cambridge – with seven men's colleges and three for women. We lived in the grounds of one of these, up against the wall of the cathedral – which was also, of course, a predominantly male society. Durham Castle was a men's college, and there was an elegant union on the Palace Green between the cathedral and the castle. This was the students' union. It housed the bar and the meeting places of the university. Access was restricted to male students, who debated there as the ones in Cambridge had done. But it was the only place where the university had any social life, as a university. In those days, as one or two of the women I met said a little bitterly, there were no real meeting places in the town; mostly pubs for miners – who also would not have appreciated the presence of women. I protested to male students I met at college gatherings. They could not see what was worrying me. Were not the Oxford and Cambridge unions single-sex? The women could build and found their own union if they wanted one.

They were perfectly pleasant young men, but blandly un-imaginative.

I taught at University College London for eleven years from 1972. I was pleased to be part of the first university in England to admit women students from its earliest days. Newnham, my college at Cambridge, had been an agnostic college. UCL, founded by Jeremy Bentham in 1826, was also agnostic, and, I imagined, politically forward-looking, rational, unprejudiced. I loved particularly the Housman Room, a staff common room and bar, large and airy, with a tree growing inside it, under a glass dome, and wonderful paintings by Slade graduates – a magnificent Stanley Spencer, a glorious Ivon Hitchens. There was a shiny modern bar, mirrored and elegant. There were other staff common rooms including the Margaret Murray Room – very small, with a teapot stand and chintzy covers on uncomfortable squat armchairs – and the Haldane Room, which I remember less well. Then I learned that until very recently these rooms had been the men's common room, the women's common room and the mixed common room. The Housman Room had, of course, been reserved for men.

I was told that my friend Isobel Armstrong had conducted a sit-in in the Housman Room in the sixties, and have always imagined her firmly and courteously refusing to leave. I have just asked her about it and she replies that she would not have had the courage to stage a sit-in but did, in her first teaching year, write a letter of complaint to the staff magazine. She later overheard a man at a Shakespeare dinner complaining that 'Some WOMAN has written to the staff magazine saying that the men's common room should be abolished. Outrageous.' She adds sadly that when she came back to London, as Professor at Birkbeck – having had chairs at Leicester and Southampton – she went into the Housman Room for the first time and was 'astonished at its luxuriance and beauty'. She adds, 'The women's common room was a little hole with a high window.'

I don't know when the segregation ended. But I do remember arguing fiercely at the Housman bar with an academic lawyer about the UCL Professors' Dining Club. This institution did not invite women professors. I – a lawyer's daughter – said this must be actionable. My interlocutor, witty and amused, said no, the Professors' Dining Club was analogous to the working men's clubs that were at the time being defended from being called discriminatory. No it wasn't, I said. If it was analogous it should at least be called the Male Professors' Dining Club. He lowered his voice slightly. He said, 'You know, they drink a lot, and then they process round the table with a huge plaster-of-Paris penis. Women wouldn't like that. It wouldn't be the same.' ∎

GRANTA

'A terrific collection of stories – mostly true ones, about families, mostly dysfunctional ones . . . All beautifully written'
William Leith, *Evening Standard*

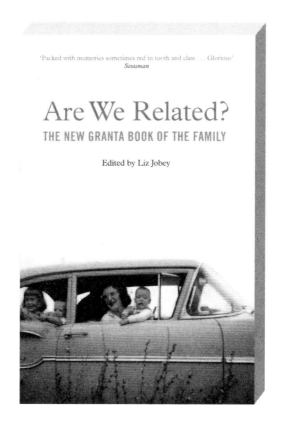

'Packed with memories sometimes red in tooth and claw . . . Glorious'
Scotsman

Are We Related?
THE NEW GRANTA BOOK OF THE FAMILY

Edited by Liz Jobey

A wonderful montage of family relationships from the past fifteen years of *Granta* magazine

Now in paperback

THE CHILDREN

Julie Otsuka

We laid them down gently, in ditches and furrows and wicker baskets beneath the trees. We left them lying naked, atop blankets, on woven straw mats at the edges of the fields. We placed them in wooden apple boxes and nursed them every time we finished hoeing a row of beans. When they were older, and more rambunctious, we sometimes tied them to chairs. We strapped them on to our backs in the dead of winter in Redding and went out to prune the grapevines, but some mornings it was so cold that their ears froze and bled. In early summer, in Stockton, we left them in nearby gullies while we dug up onions and began picking the first plums. We gave them sticks to play with in our absence and called out to them from time to time to let them know we were still there. *Don't bother the dogs. Don't touch the bees. Don't wander away or Papa will get mad.* When they tired and began to cry out for us we kept on working because if we didn't we knew we would never pay off the debt on our lease. *Mama can't come.* After a while their voices grew fainter and their crying came to a stop. And at the end of the day when there was no more light in the sky, we woke them up from wherever it was they lay sleeping and brushed the dirt from their hair. *It's time to go home.*

Some of them were stubborn and wilful and would not listen to a word we said. Others were more serene than the Buddha. *He came into the world smiling.* One loved her father more than anyone else. One hated bright colours. One would not go anywhere without his tin pail. One weaned herself at the age of thirteen months by pointing to a glass of milk on the counter and telling us, 'I want.' Several were wise beyond their years. *The fortune-teller told us he was born with the soul of an old man.* They ate at the table like grownups. They never cried. They never complained. They never left their chopsticks standing upright in their rice. They played by themselves all day long in the fields while we worked, without making a sound.

They drew pictures in the dirt for hours. And whenever we tried to pick them up and carry them home they shook their heads and said, 'I'm too heavy,' or 'Mama, rest.' They worried about us when we were tired. They worried about us when we were sad. They knew, without our telling them, when our knees were bothering us or it was our time of the month. They slept with us, at night, like puppies, on wooden boards covered with hay, and for the first time since coming to America we did not mind having someone else beside us in the bed.

Always, we had favourites. Perhaps it was our firstborn, Ichiro, who made us feel so much less lonely than we had been before. *My husband has not spoken to me in more than two years.* Or our second son, Yoichi, who taught himself how to read English by the time he was four. *He's a genius.* Or Sunoko, who always tugged at our sleeve with such fierce urgency and then forgot what it was she wanted to say. 'It will come to you later,' we would tell her, even though it never did. Some of us preferred our daughters, who were gentle and good, and some of us, like our mothers before us, preferred our sons. *They're the better gain on the farm.* We fed them more than we did their sisters. We sided with them in arguments. We dressed them in nicer clothes. We scraped up our last pennies to take them to the doctor whenever they came down with fever, while our daughters we cared for at home. *I applied a mustard plaster to her chest and said a prayer to the god of wind and bad colds.* Because we knew that our daughters would leave us the moment they married, but our sons would provide for us in our old age.

Usually, our husbands had nothing to do with them. They never changed a single diaper. They never washed a dirty dish. They never touched a broom. In the evening, no matter how tired we were when we came in from the fields, they sat down and read the paper while we cooked dinner for the children and stayed up until late washing and mending piles of clothes. They never let us go to sleep before them. They never let us rise after the sun. *You'll set a bad example for the children.* They were silent, weathered men who tramped in and out of the house in their muddy overalls muttering to themselves about sucker growth, the price of green beans, how many crates of celery they thought we could pull from the fields. They rarely spoke to their children, or even seemed to remember their names. *Tell number three boy not to slouch when he walks.* And if things grew too noisy at the table, they clapped their hands and shouted out, 'That's enough!' Their children, in turn, preferred not to speak to their fathers at all. Whenever one of them had something to say it always went through us. *Tell Papa I need a nickel. Tell Papa there's something wrong with one of the horses. Tell Papa he missed a spot shaving. Ask Papa how come he's so old.*

As soon as we could we put them to work in the fields. They picked strawberries with us in San Martin. They picked peas with us in Los Osos. They crawled behind us through the vineyards of Hughson and Del Rey as we cut down the raisin grapes and laid them out to dry on wooden trays in the sun. They hauled water. They cleared brush. They shovelled weeds. They chopped wood. They hoed in the blazing summer heat of the Imperial Valley before their bones were fully formed. Some of them were slow-moving and dreamy and planted entire rows of cauliflower sprouts upside down by mistake. Others could sort tomatoes faster than the fastest of the hired help. Many complained. They had stomach aches. Headaches. Their eyes were itching like crazy from the dust. Some of them pulled on their boots every morning without having to be told. One of them had a favourite pair of clippers, which he sharpened every evening in the barn after supper and would not let anyone else touch. One could not stop thinking about bugs. *They're everywhere.* One sat down one day in the middle of an onion patch and said she wished she'd never been born. And we wondered if we had done the right thing, bringing them into this world.

A nd yet they played for hours like calves in the fields. They made swords out of broken grape-stakes and duelled beneath the trees. They made kites out of newspaper and balsa wood and tied knives to the strings and had dogfights on windy days in the sky. They made twist-up dolls out of wire and straw and did evil things to them with sharpened chopsticks in the woods. They played shadow catch shadow on moonlit nights in the orchards, just as we had back home in Japan. They played kick the can and mumblety-peg and *jan ken po*. They had contests to see who could nail together the most packing crates the night before we went to market and who could hang the longest from the walnut tree without letting go. They folded squares of paper into airplanes and birds and watched them fly away. They collected crows' nests and snakeskins, beetle shells, acorns, rusty iron stakes from down by the tracks. They learned the names of the planets. They read each other's palms. *Your lifeline is unusually short.* They told each other's fortunes. *One day you will take a long journey on a train.* They went out into the barn after supper with their kerosene lanterns and played mama and papa in the loft. *Now slap your belly and make a sound like you're dying.* And on hot summer nights, when it was ninety-eight degrees, they spread their blankets out beneath the peach trees and dreamed of picnics down by the river, a new eraser, a book, a ball, a china doll with blinking violet eyes, leaving home, one day, for the great world beyond.

B eyond the farm, they'd heard, there were strange pale children who grew up entirely indoors and knew nothing of the fields and streams. Some of these children, they'd heard, had never even seen a tree. *Their mothers won't let them go outside and play in the sun.* Beyond the farm, they'd heard, there were fancy white houses with gold-framed mirrors and crystal doorknobs and porcelain toilets that flushed with the yank of a chain. *And they don't even make a smell.* Beyond the farm, they'd heard, there were mattresses stuffed with hard metal springs that were somehow as soft as a cloud. (Goro's sister had gone away to work as a maid in the city, and when she came back she said that the beds there were so soft she had to sleep on the floor.) Beyond the farm, they'd heard, there were mothers who ate their breakfast every morning in bed and fathers who sat on cushioned chairs all day long in their offices shouting orders into a phone – and for this, they got paid. Beyond the farm, they'd heard, wherever you went you were always a stranger and if you got on the wrong bus by mistake you might never find your way home.

They caught tadpoles and dragonflies down by the creek and put them into glass jars. They watched us kill the chickens. They found the places in the hills where the deer had last slept and lay down in their round nests in the tall, flattened grass. They pulled the tails off lizards to see how long it would take them to grow back. *Nothing's happening.* They brought home baby sparrows that had fallen from the trees and fed them sweetened rice gruel with a toothpick but in the morning, when they woke, the sparrows were dead. 'Nature doesn't care,' we told them. They sat on the fence and watched the farmer in the next field over leading his cow up to meet with the bull. They saw a mother cat eating her own kittens. 'It happens,' we explained. They heard us being taken late at night by our husbands, who would not leave us alone even though we had long ago lost our looks. 'It doesn't matter what you look like in the dark,' we were told. They bathed with us every evening, out of doors, in giant wooden tubs heated over a fire, and sank down to their chins in the hot steaming water. They leaned back their heads. They closed their eyes. They reached out for our hands. They asked us questions. *How do you know when you're dead? What if there were no birds? What if you have red spots all over your body but nothing hurts? Is it true that the Chinese really eat pigs' feet?*

They had things to keep them safe. A red bottle cap. A glass marble. A postcard of two Russian beauties strolling along the Songhua River sent to them by an uncle who was stationed in Manchuria. They had lucky white feathers that they carried with them at all times in their pockets, and stones wrapped in soft cloth that they pulled out of drawers and held – just for a moment, until the bad feeling went away – in their hands. They had secret words that they whispered to themselves whenever they felt afraid. They had favourite trees that they climbed up into whenever they wanted to be alone. *Everyone please go away.* They had favourite sisters in whose arms they could instantly fall asleep. They had hated older brothers with whom they refused to be left alone in a room. *He'll kill me.* They had dogs from whom they were inseparable and to whom they could tell all the things they could not tell anyone else. *I broke Papa's pipe and buried it under a tree.* They had their own rules. *Never sleep with your pillow facing toward the north* (Hoshiko had gone to sleep with her pillow facing north and in the middle of the night she stopped breathing and died). They had their own rituals. *You must always throw salt where a hobo has been.* They had their own beliefs. *If you see a spider in the morning you will have good luck. If you lie down after eating you will turn into a cow. If you wear a basket on your head you will stop growing. A single flower means death.*

We told them stories about tongue-cut sparrows and grateful cranes and baby doves that always remembered to let their parents perch on the higher branch. We tried to teach them manners. *Never point with your chopsticks. Never suck on your chopsticks. Never take the last piece of food from a plate.* We praised them when they were kind to others but told them not to expect to be rewarded for their good deeds. We scolded them whenever they tried to talk back. We taught them never to accept a handout. We taught them never to brag. We taught them everything we knew. *A fortune begins with a penny. It is better to suffer ill than to do ill. You must give back whatever you receive. Don't be loud like the Americans. Stay away from the Chinese. They don't like us. Watch out for the Koreans. They hate us. Be careful around the Filipinos. They're worse than the Koreans. Never marry an Okinawan. They're not real Japanese.*

In the countryside, especially, we often lost them early. To diphtheria and the measles. Tonsillitis. Whooping cough. Mysterious infections that turned gangrenous overnight. One of them was bitten by a poisonous black spider in the outhouse and came down with fever. One was kicked in the stomach by our favourite grey mule. One disappeared while we were sorting the peaches in the packing shed and even though we looked under every rock and tree for her we never did find her and after that we were never the same. *I lost the will to live.* One tumbled out of the truck while we were driving the rhubarb to market and fell into a coma from which he never awoke. One was kidnapped by a pear-picker from a nearby orchard whose advances we had repeatedly rebuffed. *I should have just told him yes.* Another was badly burned when the moonshine still exploded out back behind the barn and lived for only a day. *The last thing she said to me was, 'Mama, don't forget to look up at the sky.'* Several drowned. One in the Calaveras River. One in the Nacimiento. One in an irrigation ditch. One in a laundry tub we knew we should not have left out overnight. And every year, in August, on the Feast of the Dead, we lit white paper lanterns on their gravestones and welcomed their spirits back to Earth for a day. And at the end of that day, when it was time for them to leave, we set the paper lanterns afloat on the river to guide them safely home. For they were Buddhas now, who resided in the Land of Bliss.

A few of us were unable to have them, and this was the worst fate of all. For without an heir to carry on the family name the spirits of our ancestors would cease to exist. *I feel like I came all the way to America for nothing.* Sometimes we tried going to the faith healer, who told us that our uterus was the wrong shape and there was nothing that could be done. 'Your destiny is in the hands of the gods,' she said to us, and then she showed us to the door. Or we consulted the acupuncturist, Dr Ishida, who took one look at us and said, 'Too much yang,' and gave us herbs to nourish our yin and blood. And three months later we found ourselves miscarrying yet again. Sometimes we were sent by our husband back home to Japan, where the rumours would follow us for the rest of our lives. 'Divorced,' the neighbours would whisper. And, 'I hear she's dry as a gourd.' Sometimes we tried cutting off all our hair and offering it to the goddess of fertility if only she would make us conceive, but still, every month, we continued to bleed. And even though our husband had told us it made no difference to him whether he became a father or not – the only thing that mattered, he had said to us, was that we grew old side by side – we could not stop thinking of the children we'd never had. *Every night I can hear them playing in the fields outside my window.*

In J-Town they lived with us eight and nine to a room behind our barbershops and bathhouses and in tiny unpainted apartments that were so dark we had to leave the lights on all day long. They chopped carrots for us in our restaurants. They stacked apples for us at our fruit stands. They climbed up on to their bicycles and delivered bags of groceries to our customers' back doors. They separated the colours from the whites in our basement laundries and quickly learned to tell the difference between a red-wine stain and blood. They swept the floors of our boarding houses. They changed towels. They stripped sheets. They made up the beds. They opened doors on things that should never be seen. *I thought he was praying but he was dead.* They brought supper every evening to the elderly widow in 4A from Nagasaki, Mrs Kawamura, who worked as a chambermaid at the Hotel Drexel and had no children of her own. *My husband was a gambler who left me with only forty-five cents.* They played *go* in the lobby with the bachelor, Mr Morita, who started out as a presser at the Empress Hand Laundry thirty years ago and still worked there to this day. *It all went by so fast.* They trailed their fathers from one yard to the next as they made their gardening rounds and learned how to trim the hedges and mow the grass. They waited for us on wooden slatted benches in the park while we finished cleaning the houses across the street. *Don't talk to strangers,* we told them. *Study hard. Be patient. Whatever you do, don't end up like me.*

At school they sat in the back of the classroom in their home-made clothes with the Mexicans and spoke in timid, faltering voices. They never raised their hands. They never smiled. At recess they huddled together in a corner of the schoolyard and whispered among themselves in their secret, shameful language. In the cafeteria they were always last in line for lunch. Some of them – our firstborns – hardly knew any English and whenever they were called upon to speak their knees began to shake. One of them, when asked her name by the teacher, replied, 'Six,' and the laughter rang in her ears for days. Another said his name was Pencil, and for the rest of his life that was what he was called. Many of them begged us not to be sent back, but within weeks, it seemed, they could name all the animals in English and read aloud every sign that they saw whenever we went shopping downtown – the street of the tall timber poles, they told us, was called State Street, and the street of the unfriendly barbers was Grove, and the bridge from which Mr Itami had jumped after the stock market collapsed was the Last Chance Bridge – and wherever they went they were able to make their desires known. *One chocolate malt, please.*

One by one all the old words we had taught them began to disappear from their heads. They forgot the names of the flowers in Japanese. They forgot the names of the colours. They forgot the names of the fox god and the thunder god and the god of poverty, whom we could never escape. *No matter how long we live in this country they'll never let us buy land.* They forgot the name of the water goddess, Mizu Gami, who protected our rivers and streams and insisted that we keep our wells clean. They forgot the words for snow-light and bell cricket and fleeing in the night. They forgot what to say at the altar to our dead ancestors, who watched over us night and day. They forgot how to count. They forgot how to pray. They spent their days now living in the new language, whose twenty-six letters still eluded us even though we had been in America for years. *All I learned was the letter X so I could sign my name at the bank.* They pronounced their *L*s and *R*s with ease. And even when we sent them to the Buddhist temple on Saturdays to study Japanese they did not learn a thing. *The only reason my children go is to get out of working in the store.* But whenever we heard them talking out loud in their sleep the words that came out of their mouths came out – we were sure of it – in Japanese.

They gave themselves new names we had not chosen for them and could barely pronounce. One called herself Doris. One called herself Peggy. Many called themselves George. Saburo was called Chinky by all the others because he looked just like a Chinaman. Toshitachi was called Harlem because his skin was so dark. Etsuko was given the name Esther by her teacher, Mr Slater, on her first day of school. 'It's his mother's name,' she explained. To which we replied, 'So is yours.' Sumire called herself Violet. Shizuko was Sugar. Makoto was just Mac. Shigeharu Takagi joined the Methodist Church at the age of nine and changed his name to Paul. Edison Kobayashi was born lazy but had a photographic memory and could tell you the name of every person he'd ever met. Grace Sugita didn't like ice cream. *Too cold.* Kitty Matsutaro expected nothing and got nothing in return. Six-foot-four Tiny Honda was the biggest Japanese we'd ever seen. Mop Yamasaki had long hair and liked to dress like a girl. Lefty Hayashi was the star pitcher at Emerson Junior High. Sam Nishimura had been sent to Tokyo to receive a proper Japanese education and had just returned to America after six and a half years. *They made him start all over again in the first grade.* Daisy Takada had perfect posture and liked to do things in sets of four. Mabel Ota's father had gone bankrupt three times. Lester Nakano's family bought all their clothes at the Goodwill. Tommy Takayama's mother was – everyone knew it – a whore. *She has six different children by five different men. And two of them are twins.*

Soon we could barely recognize them. They were taller than we were, and heavier. They were loud beyond belief. *I feel like a duck that's hatched goose's eggs.* They preferred their own company to ours and pretended not to understand a word that we said. Our daughters took big long steps, in the American manner, and moved with undignified haste. They wore their garments too loose. They swayed their hips like mares. They chattered away like coolies the moment they came home from school and said whatever popped into their minds. *Mr Dempsey has a folded ear.* Our sons grew enormous. They insisted on eating bacon and eggs every morning for breakfast instead of bean-paste soup. They refused to use chopsticks. They drank gallons of milk. They poured ketchup all over their rice. They spoke perfect English just like on the radio and whenever they caught us bowing before the kitchen god in the kitchen and clapping our hands they rolled their eyes and said, 'Mama, *please.*'

Mostly, they were ashamed of us. Our floppy straw hats and threadbare clothes. Our heavy accents. *Every sing oh righ?* Our cracked, calloused palms. Our deeply lined faces black from years of picking peaches and staking grape plants in the sun. They longed for real fathers with briefcases who went to work in a suit and tie and only mowed the grass on Sundays. They wanted different and better mothers who did not look so worn out. *Can't you put on a little lipstick?* They dreaded rainy days in the country when we came to pick them up after school in our old battered pickups. They never invited friends over to our crowded homes in J-Town. *We live like beggars.* They would not be seen with us at the temple on the Emperor's birthday. They would not celebrate the annual Freeing of the Insects with us at the end of summer in the park. They refused to join hands and dance with us in the streets on the Festival of the Autumnal Equinox. They laughed at us whenever we insisted that they bow to us first thing in the morning and with each passing day they seemed to slip further and further from our grasp.

Some of them developed unusually good vocabularies and became the best students in the class. They won prizes for best essay on California wild flowers. They received highest honours in science. They had more gold stars than anyone else on the teacher's chart. Others fell behind every year during harvest season and had to repeat the same grade twice. One got pregnant at fourteen and was sent away to live with her grandparents on a silkworm farm in remote western Japan. *Every week she writes to me asking when she can come home.* One took his own life. Several quit school. A few ran wild. They formed their own gangs. They made up their own rules. *No knives. No girls. No Chinese allowed.* They went around late at night looking for other people to fight. *Let's go beat up some Filipinos.* And when they were too lazy to leave the neighbourhood they stayed at home and fought among themselves. *You goddamn Jap!* Others kept their heads down and tried not to be seen. They went to no parties (they were invited to no parties). They played no instruments. They never got valentines (they never sent valentines). They didn't like to dance (they didn't have the right shoes). They floated ghostlike through the halls, with their eyes turned away and their books clutched to their chests, as though lost in a dream. If someone called them a name behind their back they did not hear it. If someone called them a name to their face they just nodded and walked on. If they were given the oldest textbooks to use in math class they shrugged and took it in stride. *I never really liked algebra anyway.* If their pictures appeared at the end of the yearbook they pretended not to mind. 'That's just the way it is,' they said to themselves. And, 'So what?' And, 'Who cares?' Because they knew that no matter what they did they would never really fit in.

They learned which mothers would let them come over (Mrs Henke, Mrs Woodruff, Mrs Alfred Chandler III) and which would not (all the other mothers). They learned which barbers would cut their hair (the Negro barbers) and which barbers to avoid (the grumpy barbers on the south side of Grove). They learned that there were certain things that would never be theirs: higher noses, fairer complexions, longer legs that might be noticed from afar. *Every morning I do my stretching exercises but it doesn't seem to help.* They learned when they could go swimming at the YMCA – *Coloured days are on Mondays* – and when they could go to the picture show at the Pantages Theater downtown (never). They learned that they should always call the restaurant first. *Do you serve Japanese?* They learned not to go out alone during the daytime and what to do if they found themselves cornered in an alley after dark. *Just tell them you know judo.* And if that didn't work, they learned to fight back with their fists. *They respect you when you're strong.* They learned to find protectors. They learned to hide their anger. *No, of course. I don't mind. That's fine. Go ahead.* They learned never to show their fear. They learned that some people are born luckier than others and that things in this world do not always go as you plan.

Still, they dreamed. One swore she would one day marry a preacher so she wouldn't have to pick berries on Sundays. One wanted to save up enough money to buy his own farm. One wanted to become a tomato-grower like his father. One wanted to become anything but. One wanted to plant a vineyard. One wanted to start his own label. *I'd call it Fukuda Orchards.* One could not wait until the day she got off the ranch. One wanted to go to college even though no one she knew had ever left the town. *I know it's crazy, but . . .* One loved living out in the country and never wanted to leave. *It's better here. Nobody knows who we are.* One wanted something more but could not say exactly what it was. *This just isn't enough.* One wanted a Swing King drum set with hi-hat cymbals. One wanted a spotted pony. One wanted his own paper route. One wanted her own room, with a lock on the door. *Anyone who came in would have to knock first.* One wanted to become an artist and live in a garret in Paris. One wanted to go to refrigeration school. *You can do it through the mail.* One wanted to build bridges. One wanted to play the piano. One wanted to operate his own fruit stand alongside the highway instead of working for somebody else. One wanted to learn shorthand at the Merritt Secretarial Academy and get an inside job in an office. *Then I'd have it made.* One wanted to become the next Great Togo on the professional wrestling circuit. One wanted to become a state senator. One wanted to cut hair and open her own salon. One had polio and just wanted to breathe without her iron lung. One wanted to become a master seamstress. One wanted to become a teacher. One wanted to become a doctor. One wanted to become his sister. One wanted to become a gangster. One wanted to become a star. And even though we saw the darkness coming we said nothing and let them dream on. ■

GRANTA

A TRAIN IN WINTER

Caroline Moorehead

JEANETTE L'HERMINIER

Douchka Hamelot and ML Flandin – known as Laurette – have lunch together

Drawing signed by the models

Pencil on newspaper, 13.5 cm x 13.5 cm

© Musée de la Résistance et de la Déportation de Besançon

In early spring 1942, in a crackdown on the French Resistance that would become known as *L'Affaire Pican*, the French police dealt what they called a decisive blow to the Resistance. Their haul included three million anti-German and anti-Vichy tracts, three tonnes of paper, two typewriters, eight roneo machines, 1,000 stencils, 100 kilos of ink and 300,000 francs. One hundred and thirteen people were detained, thirty-five of them women. The youngest of these was a sixteen-year-old schoolgirl called Rosa Floch, who was picked up as she was writing *Vive les anglais!* on the walls of her *lycée*. The eldest was a forty-four-year-old farmer's wife, Madeleine Normand, who told the police that the 39,500 francs in her handbag were there because she had recently sold a horse.

Nine months later, on the snowy morning of 24 January 1943, these women – along with others arrested like them in raids across occupied France – were transported on the only train to take women from the French Resistance to the Nazi death camps during the entire four years of German occupation.

It was not the cold that hit the women as the cattle-truck doors were pulled back in the pale light of a Silesian dawn; they were cold already, so cold that almost all feeling had left their bodies. It was the noise. The first sounds were shouts, orders rattled out, fierce and rapid, the German words incomprehensible but the meaning – to hurry, to move, to climb down, to get into line, to leave the heavier suitcases – was plain. More frightening were the sounds made by the dogs, snarling, growling, barking as they pulled on their leads to get at the women.

One by one, helping each other, putting out a steadying hand, clutching one another's shoulders, trying not to fall or to panic, the 230 women climbed down on to rough ground, fearful and confused.

They felt weak from lack of food and their mouths were parched from thirst. All around them stretched an enormous frozen plain, with trees in the distance. Deep snow that looked as grey as the immense sky above lay as far as the eye could see. Stiff and shocked, huddling close together, they shuffled into ragged lines of five, one behind the other, as ordered by the shouting soldiers. Among the SS men with guns were a number of women in long black capes, with hoods high above military caps and tall black-leather boots. The SS had truncheons and whips. The platform, with its single line, stood out in the countryside on its own; there were no buildings, no station.

The order was given to march. One of the women, Marie-Claude Vaillant-Couturier (a journalist who had written about Dachau in the 1930s and the first to fall into the hands of the *brigades spéciales* on 4 February 1942), spoke good German. She translated, and her words were repeated back down the line. As they moved off across the icy, slippery, uneven ground in their thin shoes, they saw approaching in the half-light a group of women who seemed to belong to another world, emaciated, stumbling, their heads shaven and wearing a grotesque assortment of ill-fitting clothes, most of them striped. The smell the women gave off was repugnant, unidentifiable. Lulu Serre, a young factory worker who had helped hide and distribute tracts for the Resistance, remarked to her neighbours, 'How filthy they are. They could at least wash.'

A little further on they encountered a party of thin, ragged men, wearing the same striped clothes. None replied to their calls. As they walked, Jacqueline Quatremaire (a young secretary who had been followed by the police for three months before being arrested for her role in typing up Resistance tracts) began to sing the Marseillaise, soon picked up by a twenty-three-year-old locksmith's daughter called Raymonde Salez (who had taken part in an attack on the German bookshop in Paris) and then, in ones and twos, by the others. The women straightened their shoulders and tried to stand taller. So it was that, singing loudly, the 230 women approached the double rows of barbed wire and the watchtowers and passed under the sign that said *Arbeit Macht Frei* and into the camp, where other women, amazed to hear such sounds, opened the windows of their huts to listen. The Frenchwomen had no idea where they were, though Marie-Claude had translated a sign nailed to a post spotted along the way: *Vernichtungslager.* '*Nichts*,' she said, 'nothing, nothingness, towards nothing.' Had they heard the words Auschwitz or Birkenau, these too would have meant nothing to them.

By the time the Frenchwomen arrived in Birkenau, the camp's dual activities were just reaching their full potential. Every new train, for the most part filled with Jews from the ghettos of Holland, France, Belgium, Greece, Germany, Yugoslavia, Czechoslovakia, Poland and Italy, brought a small number – perhaps 10 to 15 per cent of the total – of people judged fit enough to be worked to death. The rest – the elderly, the infirm, the children, the women with babies or who were pregnant – were sent straight from the railway siding to the gas chambers.

Four new crematoria, built by Topf and Sons, were almost completed, together with underground undressing rooms, which would not only vastly speed up the process of extermination – in theory 4,416 people would be 'processed' every twenty-four hours – but remove the smell of burning flesh that hung over the surrounding countryside. Under the new streamlined system, teams of *Sonderkommando** prisoners loaded the ovens, having extracted the gold from teeth for shipment back to the Reichsbank in ingots, shorn the hair for later use as felt and thread, removed the ashes from the grates and taken the crushed residue by lorry to the River Vistula. The forty-fourth transport of French Jews from Drancy reached Birkenau shortly before the arrival of the Frenchwomen. All but a very few of the people who had been on board had already been gassed. Plans were now pushing ahead to receive the

---

* The name given to teams of male prisoners, kept separate and alive to work the crematoria, before themselves being gassed and incinerated.

Gypsy populations of occupied Europe.

Alongside its function as a death and labour camp, Birkenau, since the late spring of 1942, had been the main women's camp in the Auschwitz complex. Here, in January 1943, were living some 15,000 women from every corner of Europe, in conditions worse than those in all other parts of the camp. There was appalling overcrowding, a chronic lack of water, and latrines that were no more than open concrete sewers deep in mud and excrement. Together with endemic typhus, dysentery, tuberculosis, scabies and impetigo, the women suffered from abscesses that seemed never to heal. Already severely malnourished, they were dying at the rate of about a fifth of their number every month. Debilitated, covered in sores, their limbs bloated, they inhabited a world in which all normal patterns of behaviour had broken down, in which men and women of the SS, free of constraints, exercised a reign of violence, corruption and depersonalization, in which not to steal or to lie would most likely result in death, and in which the worst traits to be found in human beings, not their best ones, were rewarded. And over them presided a hierarchy of female *Kapos*: inmate supervisors and *Blockältester*, 'block elders', for the most part German criminal prisoners who effectively collaborated with the SS and whose own survival depended on brutality. Their viciousness and vindictiveness was said to surpass by far that of their male counterparts.

It was in this version of hell that the 230 Frenchwomen, some of them in their late fifties or early sixties, others still schoolgirls, accustomed to having enough to eat, warm beds to sleep in, clean clothes and the civility and decency of strangers, now found themselves.

There was no heat in the barracks into which they were led but after their agonizingly cold, faltering, slithering walk, they were pleased to sit down, even if all they could find to sit on were the edges of stone and wood-slatted bunks that rose in tiers to the ceiling. At midday two prisoners in striped clothes arrived with a cauldron of hot liquid, a thin gruel-like soup made of grasses; red enamel bowls were handed out. Not everyone drank the soup, saying that the bowls had a fetid, sickening smell, and that they would prefer to wait for the bread. There was no bread, they were told, and they would do better to eat whatever came their way. They learned later that the smell came from the fact that in the other barracks the women, suffering from dysentery, could not always reach the latrines in the night and used the bowls instead. As the Frenchwomen hesitated, the Germans and the Poles who had already been in the barracks when they arrived pressed forwards, fighting each other to get at the soup.

At one point, the doors to the barracks opened and a group of SS men entered. One stepped forward and asked whether there was a dentist among them, the camp dentist having recently died. Danielle Casanova put her hand up and was led out.

After this began the process of induction into the life of Birkenau. The women's names were called out, with Marie-Claude acting as interpreter. They were told to undress, to put their clothes and all their other belongings including any photographs of their families into their cases and mark these with their names. They were led into a room where other prisoners were waiting with scissors to cut their hair, getting as close to the scalp as possible. Their pubic hair was also clipped and another woman wiped the shorn and bald parts with a rag dipped in petrol as a disinfectant. When it came to the turn of eighteen-year-old Hélène Brabander (whose doctor father François and brother Romuald had been unloaded from the train at Sachsenhausen), her mother, Sophie, took the scissors and cut her daughter's hair herself. Janine Herschel, one of the very few Jews on the train – though, having used a false certificate of baptism, no one knew that she was Jewish – offered an SS guard her gold watch, studded with diamonds, in return for sparing her bleached, blonde hair. The SS man took the watch and Janine's hair was chopped off anyway.

As there was not enough water for a shower they were next led, naked, into a room full of steam. Some of the women had never taken their clothes off in front of strangers. They shrank back as SS guards, men and women, came in and laughed at their naked bodies. The young Simone Sampaix, looking around desperately for a face she recognized among the bald heads, heard Cécile Charua (known as le Cygne d'Enghien, she had been a highly efficient courier and liaison officer for the printing underground) call out: 'Come here, come and sit with us.'

After this came the tattoo, a series of pricks, each woman's number taken from the transport on which she reached the camp – theirs was the transport of the 31,000 – traced on the inside of their lower left arm by a French Jewish prisoner, who assured them that it would not hurt. They felt they were being branded, like cattle. Charlotte Delbo, who had returned to Paris from Argentina and joined the Resistance effort as a translator with the underground press, became number 31,661; Cécile 31,650; Madeleine Passot (known to her friends as Betty) 31,668. The 230 women, forever after, would be known as *le convoi des 31,000.*

Next, still naked, they were led into yet another room, this one full of what looked like rags piled up on the floor, where other prisoners were waiting to issue each woman with a sleeveless vest, a pair of grey knickers reaching to the knees, a scarf, a dress, a jacket and rough grey socks and stockings without elastic. The outer garments were all made of the same striped material. They took what they were given, regardless of size, the large women crammed into small dresses, the small enveloped in sack-like jackets. Worse, the clothes were filthy, spotted with blood and pus and faeces, and damp from some rudimentary attempts at disinfection. When Simone's turn came to get shoes, all that were left were clogs, with a band of material roughly nailed over the top, which meant that her toes and heels were bare. It made walking hard. Madeleine Doiret (Mado) got slippers of torn felt.

Their last task was to sew on to each jacket and dress their personal numbers, as well as an F, for French, and a red triangle. Asking what this meant, they were told that it denoted their status as political prisoners, those held for 'anti-German activities', and that they would do well to learn the meaning of the other symbols: green for the criminal prisoners; purple for the Jehovah's Witnesses; black for the 'asocials'; pink for homosexuals; a six-pointed Star of David for the Jews. Some prisoners wore a combination of symbols – as Jews, 'race defilers', recidivists and criminals.

The women discovered that they were regarded as 'dangerous', and that the other prisoners had been ordered to turn their backs as they passed by. A Dutchwoman in the sewing room asked: 'How many are you?' Told that there were 230 of them, she said: 'In a month, there will only be thirty of you.' She herself, she added, had been one of a thousand women arriving on a train from Holland in October; now she was the only one left alive. Had the others been executed? No, she replied, they died after the roll calls, hours and hours standing still in the snow and ice. It was easier, more comforting, not to believe her.

When the Frenchwomen left to return to the barracks, the icy cold had frozen their damp clothes stiff.

Block 14, where the women were taken (to their immense relief all together), was a quarantine block; it was here that they would spend the first fortnight in Birkenau, though one morning they were marched over to the men's camp to be photographed and measured. Spared the work details that later would take them to the factories, brickyards and marshes, they were not let off the roll calls; all too soon, they understood the Dutchwoman's warning. At half past three in the morning, long before it grew light, every woman in the camp was harried out of her bunk and barracks by *Kapos* with whips, to stand in the gluey mud and snow to await the arrival of the SS to count them.

From the first, the Frenchwomen clung together, in groups, each slipping her hands under the arms of the woman in front, the rows constantly changing place so that no one spent too long on the outside. 'We held on to each other,' Madeleine Dissoubray would later say. 'If someone was particularly cold, we just kept them in the middle.' Using Charlotte's watch, they decided they would swap places every fifteen minutes. To deal with the extreme cold, Charlotte tried to pretend she was somewhere else, to recite poems to herself in order 'to remain me', but the reality of the cold and exhaustion was often too overwhelming.

At dawn, the count began. When the numbers did not tally, the counting started again. The rows had to be neat, the squares of women perfectly formed; the guards shouted, shoved, dealt out blows. Roll calls could last several hours and were repeated at the end of each day. It was impossible to clean off the mud and excrement clinging to the women's feet; mud haunted their dreams. To fall during roll call would mean death, for there was no way to clean or change and the wet muddy clothes froze on their backs. To lose shoes could also bring death, for there were no replacements. Those spotted barefoot were often sent straight to the gas chambers, women being easier to replace than shoes.

It was clear that not all would, or could, or would choose to, survive. A look of death became imprinted on some of their faces. The camp was too degrading, too shocking for some of the women to bear. Using the latrines meant wading through excrement and crouching over a long open sewer, trying not to fall in. Accustomed to order and predictability, they had neither the strength nor the desire to adjust to a world whose rules were so arbitrary and so barbaric.

What was clear to the younger, stronger women, particularly those who, like Cécile, were used to hard lives and the discipline of the Communist Party, was that in order to survive they would have to take some kind of control over what was happening to them. They could not, they told each other, become victims, vulnerable to every twist of chance. They needed to organize themselves, to understand their surroundings, to navigate the dangers and respond quickly enough to the orders shouted at them in the camp jargon, with its mixture of Polish, Yiddish, Silesian and German.

On the third morning, returning from the roll call stiff, cold and hungry, Charlotte suggested that the women do gymnastics together. It would make them strong, they agreed, and give them energy and hope. Forcing their companions outside to jump and stretch, they were seen by a group of other women, themselves on their way to a work detail. 'You must be mad,' one of them called out. 'Don't use up your energy. You are going to need it.' Mai Politzer, who had been a courier and typist for the underground, tried to start folk dances. The women knew they looked absurd, as Dr Adelaide Hautval, a doctor from Strasbourg who had been picked up for defending a family of Jews, later wrote. They shuffled awkwardly around in their striped clothes, 'but it gave us a feeling of being ourselves'.

In early 1943 work was continuing on the expansion of the camp: there were still buildings to be knocked down and cleared and the marshes were being drained for agricultural projects. On the first morning, the women were walked, for almost two hours, in their lines of five – the guards shouting *'Links! Zwei! Drei!'* – holding one another's arms so as not to slip on the ice in their ill-fitting shoes. To keep up their spirits, they sang. It was so foggy that Charlotte Delbo kept worrying they would become separated. Those whose swollen legs made walking difficult were supported by the others.

When they reached a swampy field they were given shovels and hoes, and wheelbarrows without wheels which were loaded with mud and stones and carried to a ditch to be emptied. All day, except for a pause in the late morning when a tepid, thin soup of swedes and cabbage arrived, they dug through the ice, lifted and shovelled, staggering and falling under the weight. With the temperature far below zero, the metal handles stuck to their sweaty palms.

When a pale sun rose and the ice began to melt, their feet sank ever deeper into the mud so that they were soon standing ankle-deep in mud and water. Women unaccustomed to physical work, whose lives had been spent in offices or schoolrooms, found it acutely painful. Their backs, arms and legs ached. The SS guards, well fed and warmly dressed, lit fires around which they crouched, and if the women paused in their work, they sent the dogs over to snap at their heels, or came themselves to deal out blows. From all over the misty field could be heard shouts and cries of pain. Charlotte, watching the rows of toiling women, thought they looked like ants, 'a frieze of shadows against the light'. The shovels grew heavier and heavier. The women felt feverish. At dusk, when the whistle blew to stop work, it was found that every Frenchwoman had survived the day. Not all the Poles had, and they had to wait for the bodies of the dead to be collected. Then came the two-hour walk back to camp and the evening roll call. It was dark by the time they returned to their barracks.

Half a litre of black coffee in the morning, watery soup at midday, 300 grams of bread – if they were lucky – with either a scrape of margarine, a bit of sausage, cheese or jam at night, was not enough to stop the women's bodies from shrinking and feeding on themselves, the fat disappearing first and then the muscles. The food never varied. It left the prisoners famished, bloated and constantly needing to urinate, their stomachs swollen as if pregnant. Cécile continued to say that it was not as bad for her, since she had grown up poor and spent most of her childhood hungry, but Marie Alizon, who had arrived in Birkenau a healthy, energetic young woman, was tormented by cravings for food.

But it was thirst rather than hunger that haunted Charlotte; agonizing, unceasing thirst that made her jaws lock and her teeth feel as if they were glued to her cheeks. The women's camp had just one tap for 12,000 prisoners, and it was fiercely guarded by the green triangles, the German criminal prisoners. Charlotte became increasingly obsessed. To the horror and fear of the others, walking one morning towards the marshes, she left the line and went over to a brook to lick the ice. The guards did not see her. Later, she drank the muddy water of the marshes. At night, back in the barracks, she exchanged her small portion of bread for a mug of tea. She dreamed of oranges, the juice flowing down her throat.

Then came the day when, assigned to a tree-planting detail, her desperation was such that she feared she was going mad. That night, her friends pooled all their bread for an entire bucket of water. When they gave it to her, Charlotte plunged her head in, rather like a horse, and drank until she reached the bottom. Her stomach swelled alarmingly. But in some miraculous way, she was cured. The obsession lifted. She would later say that when she had thought of suicide, she rejected it. In a place of such constant death, the immediate aim became not to die but to live, to get enough to eat and drink, to keep warm. That was all she thought about.

By now the Frenchwomen were no longer under any illusion about the smoke that rose from the chimneys at the far end of the camp and filled their mouths, throats and lungs with a cloying, nauseating taste. They could see for themselves the way the chimneys belched out flames about three-quarters of an hour after the arrival of a Jewish transport. What haunted Marie-Elisa Nordmann (a Jewish scientist) was the thought that her mother might be on one of the trains. When they now saw the lorries carrying the dead and the dying from Block 25, they knew that those still alive would be thrown straight into the flames along with the dead. 'It was a ceaseless battle,' Madeleine Dissoubray would say, 'with ourselves, not to give up.'

Cécile felt guilty when walking back from long days in the marshes: when she could smell the acrid smoke she was relieved, knowing that they no longer had far to walk. At night, she dreamed of the smell, which made her think of the boiled-down carcasses of animals. Looking around at her emaciated and sickly companions, knowing that most would soon be dead, she kept seeing herself in the mound of corpses. 'I don't know if anyone else felt hope,' she said later. 'But I never did.' She rarely wept, she would later say, because she was in such a permanent state of horror that tears rarely came.

March brought rains. The snow melted and the marshes turned into a sea of mud. Those responsible for collecting the vast cauldrons of soup sank in that sea up to their thighs. Sixty-seven days after reaching Birkenau, the women removed their stockings for the first time and were permitted to wash their feet in the water now flowing in the ditches. They discovered that except for their big toes, all their other nails had gone. Looking at her friends sitting in the dust and dried mud reminded Charlotte of a 'miserable swarm that made one think of flies on a dungheap'.

She dreamed of having three baths, one after the other, in warm, soft, soapy water. During the interminable roll calls, the women had taken to playing a game. One would ask another: 'If you could choose between a big bowl of boiling hot, foamy chocolate, or a bath with lavender soap, or a warm cosy bed, which would you choose?' Nearly always, the answer was either the hot bath or the warm bed.

But the number of survivors was dwindling. Dysentery had set in and the women aged before the eyes of their friends. Typhus, brought to Auschwitz in April 1941 by prisoners transferred from a jail in Lublin, was ravaging the camp. One by one the Frenchwomen, who had survived the hunger, the backbreaking work, the intense cold and the endless skin infections, began to fall ill. At roll call they pinched their ashen cheeks to appear healthier. All night, death rattles could be heard rising from the bunks. Women woke to find that their faces had swollen during the night and that they were too ill to move. They were now dying at the same rate as the Jewish women, who were more brutally treated by the guards. On one single night, nine of the remaining Frenchwomen died.

The younger girls did not appear to possess the resilience of the older women. Even when physically strong and capable, they seemed to be mentally more fragile, thus more vulnerable. Twenty-year-old Andrée Tamisé was already weakened by dysentery when she picked up a chest infection. Desperate not to be parted from her sister Gilberte, she dragged herself, with Gilberte's help, to the marshes. Each day, she found breathing a little harder. Finally one morning, she said to Gilberte, 'I can't follow you any more.' When the others left for work, she tried to join the line of women queuing by the *Revier* (the infirmary), but a guard pushed her away. Andrée crept back into her bunk and hid. But a *Kapo* spotted her, dragged her outside and beat her. That night Gilberte returned to find her sister covered in mud, bruised and semi-conscious. During the night, Andrée died. Rising before dawn next morning, Gilberte carried her body outside and laid it tenderly by a wall.

Two and a half months after reaching Birkenau, the number of Frenchwomen was down to eighty. A hundred and fifty of them had died: from typhus, pneumonia, dysentery, from dog bites and beatings and gangrenous frostbite, from not being able to eat or sleep, or from being gassed. In the filth and cold and danger of Birkenau, almost anything was fatal. The ones still alive were the stronger women, those neither too old nor too young, those sustained by belief in a new world order or, quite simply, those who had been lucky. Without one another's help, they knew that many more of them would already be dead. One Sunday, when the sky was blue and the women were allowed to rest, Charlotte remembered other spring Sundays, when she would walk by the Seine under the chestnut trees. 'None of us,' she thought, 'none of us will return.'

What was now absolutely plain to the eighty Frenchwomen, many of whom were extremely frail, was that their survival would depend on great luck and on their ability to adapt and organize themselves. They had taken care to master enough German and the bastardized language of the camps to react quickly to orders and so avoid blows that would come from any perceived hesitation. They had learned to hang back when the cauldrons of soup arrived, in order to get the bottom layers where shreds of meat or vegetables gathered. They knew to cultivate friends in 'Canada' (the name given to the repository of the possessions looted from Jews deported to Auschwitz), where, in return for extra portions of bread, these friends might take the risk of stealing a pair of woollen stockings or some decent shoes. They had discovered how important it was to stay together, not get separated, so each could watch the others' backs.

Their own particular skills as women – caring for others and being practical – made them, they told themselves, less vulnerable than men to harsh conditions and despair. Adaptability was crucial, resignation fatal. The inability to undo a vision of life as it should be and not cope with what it was led, as they had observed, to apathy and the condition of those more dead than alive. Along with the other camp survivors, they did their best to stay clean, to wash their faces in the snow or icy brooks, believing that it made them both healthier and more dignified. And they wanted, passionately, to live, to survive the war and to describe to the world exactly what they had been through and what they had witnessed.

When Germaine Pican found a dead crow in the marshes, even the mouthful she shared with the others gave them a sense of achievement. Charlotte, for her part, fought the cold and exhaustion by pretending that she was somewhere else, reciting poems and plays to herself. Her refrain was 'to keep alive, to remain me'. It did not nullify what was going on around her, but it made her feel some kind of 'victory over horror'.

Even so, by May most of the women had ceased in their hearts to believe they would live to see the end of the war. Conditions in the women's camp at Birkenau, worse than elsewhere in Auschwitz, with more overcrowding and less water, were getting harsher, and few felt confident that they could for much longer escape the sudden and arbitrary brutality of the SS and the *Kapos*. Their bodies were covered in soft, fat, white lice. They were exhausted. Walking back at the end of a long day in the marshes, Cécile, so strong and positive by nature, could only think how close she felt to the end, how she was without hope of any kind.

In Ukraine and Belorussia, the Germans had seen fields of *koksaghyz*, a dandelion from central Asia whose root and juice contained latex, and from which the Russians derived rubber. In desperate need of rubber themselves, the Germans thought they could cultivate *koksaghyz* on the swampy plains of Auschwitz and appointed Joachim Caesar, an SS *Obersturmbannführer* with a PhD in agricultural sciences, to run the laboratory.

The first recruits chosen to work under him were Polish women from Birkenau, but in March word reached Marie-Claude, whose position in the camp administration meant she was aware of any new developments, that Caesar was looking for biologists. Marie-Elisa Nordmann and Madeleine Dechavassina, both chemists before the war, applied. Marie-Elisa was actually in the infirmary with pneumonia and had such a high temperature that she could not stand up, but a nurse showed her how to bring the fever down with an instant remedy of 90 per cent alcohol and a bit of coffee, and she pulled round before the medical inspection. And in the wake of Marie-Elisa and Madeleine, claiming scientific expertise that few had any notion of, fifteen more Frenchwomen were allowed to join for the experimental station at Raisko. Among them were Cécile, Charlotte, Germaine Pican, Lulu and her sister Carmen. Lulu would later say that up until that moment, she had barely been able to tell a potato from a carrot.

Raisko, which consisted of an old schoolhouse surrounded by fields and greenhouses, lay some three kilometres from Birkenau. It was encircled by barbed wire but not electrified, and there were no watchtowers with SS guards and guns. Caesar, who was afraid of contagion, as were all the SS, and whose own wife had died of typhus not long before, insisted that the women who worked for him were clean and healthy. After nearly three months of filth, the Frenchwomen could not believe it when they were permitted to wash and were given clean new blouses and proper leather shoes; though the food was the same, the soup was thicker, and there were endless possibilities of 'organizing' – Auschwitz's word for stealing – vegetables from the surrounding fields, where other prisoners were growing produce for the SS.

Until a new barracks was made ready for them, the women returned to Birkenau each night. The camp still lay under a crust of ice, and when the moon shone the barbed wire was picked out in frost. They tramped through a silent, still world, holding on to one another, so as not to slip. But then they moved into Raisko dormitories where each woman had her own bed, with a straw mattress. There were hot showers. The roll call, during which so many of their friends had died, was reduced to no more than a few minutes morning and evening. There were far fewer fleas. Caesar was more interested in getting results – which would keep him from a possible transfer to the Eastern front – than in persecuting his staff. At times he treated the scientists among them almost as colleagues. Their ailments were even noted in the ledger of the Raisko hospital, where they were allowed to spend time when ill. When it got warmer one of the SS guards, who told the women that unless he was soon transferred away from Auschwitz he was going to kill himself, let them bathe in a pond and wash their clothes, while he looked scrupulously away.

The work was not arduous. The more skilled among them, such as Marie-Elisa and Madeleine, were assigned to a young German chemist called Ruth Weimann in the laboratory, where they divided their time between helping her with the chemistry for her dissertation, and ensuring that the results of their experiments appeared positive, the better to prolong Raisko's existence. The others worked in the *koksaghyz* fields, sorted plants and acted as assistants. Occasionally, they were ordered to make funeral wreaths for SS guards who died of typhus. On arriving, Marie-Elisa had discovered a friend and colleague from before the war, Claudette Bloch, who told her that several of the Frenchmen from *le convoi des 45,000* (the men of the French Resistence transported to Birkenau in July 1942) were employed at Raisko as gardeners. As in Birkenau, the men had found ways of learning the news, and even of getting hold of newspapers, which they now left hidden in safe spots for the women. Using an atlas from 'Canada', concealed in an attic above the laboratory, Marie-Elisa, Charlotte and the others were able to follow the Nazi defeats on the Eastern front.

When Caesar married Ruth Weimann, the women were ordered to make a duvet for the bridal pair out of the feathers from the geese and ducks reared not far away for the SS. They took great pleasure in leaving in some of the sharper quills. With the food and warmth had come a new taste for life. Women whose horizons had shrunk to an hourly preoccupation with survival found themselves once again wanting diversion. They began to barter, taught by the Polish women who had become skilled at negotiating for cabbages, potatoes and beans with the Russian prisoner gardeners. They discovered that extra bread, saved from their own rations, could be swapped for a lump of sugar, a packet of noodles, or even needles, thread and pens. To see their friends slowly come back to life, looking less haunted and skeletal, beginning to smile again, was a delight for each of them. When one day the SS came and confiscated everything from their barracks, the women gathered together and sang the Marseillaise, very softly, under their breaths. Next day they set about replacing everything they had lost.

On the pretext that the nearby Institute of Hygiene, where some of the Frenchmen were working, had more sophisticated equipment and that they needed access to this in order to centrifuge their latex samples, Marie-Elisa and Hélène were able to make contact with the male prisoners. They hid tomatoes in their voluminous knickers and exchanged them for jam. It was very risky, for all such transactions were strictly forbidden, but it gave them a feeling that they were not entirely without power. It also inspired them to perform small acts of sabotage, selecting the weaker roots for propagation, mixing up the numbers of batches and treating the plants with chemicals to stunt their growth. The women had become skilled at thieving. Charlotte Decock, who was sent to join the others in Raisko as cook for the SS, stole everything she could lay her hands on – wine, flour, eggs, a jar of pickled pork – though getting rid of the jar afterwards proved almost impossible.

In the evenings, while sitting on their beds, the friends sewed and drew and even did embroidery and discussed how they might find ways of making borscht, and how delicious it would be if they could only get hold of some cream. They might have become bolder in their scavenging had Germaine Pican not been caught trying to smuggle onions back to their friends in Birkenau, and sent back there herself as punishment. Though he encouraged the women to do what they could to improve their surroundings and even once found sunglasses for those working in the fields, Caesar did not intervene over punishments. Nor did he save a young girl called Lily, who had a fiancé among the gardeners and who was shot when a note of his was intercepted. 'We are like plants full of life and sap, like plants wanting to grow and live,' the boy had written, 'and I cannot help thinking that these plants are not meant to live.'

The autumn brought no further deaths to the Frenchwomen left behind at Birkenau. A hundred and seventy-seven had died in a little over six months. Those who remained were determined, capable women, very strong mentally as well as physically; it was no accident that all but a few of the survivors had been active politically, committed to shared beliefs in a better future, and accustomed to hardship and discipline. They were all much the same age, in their late twenties and early thirties. Poupette and Simone were the only young girls still alive; all the older women were dead, without exception. Of the forty-seven women of the Resistance rounded up in the raids of 1942, fewer than ten remained alive. The dead included most of the *résistance intellectuelle* from Paris, almost all the printers and many of the young women who had handed out leaflets for the *jeunes filles de France*.

There had been some changes in Auschwitz. After a scandal involving excessive pilfering of 'Canada' by the SS, Rudolf Hoess, commandant, had been replaced by a slightly less savage man. Arthur Liebehenschel set about curbing the corruption and transferring out of Auschwitz guards he regarded as too brutal and when the work commandos returned from the factories and marshes in the evenings, they began to bring fewer corpses back with them. Liebehenschel was particularly fond of music, and he liked to have an orchestra of women prisoners, many of them distinguished musicians, playing on all possible occasions, dressed in matching pleated skirts and white blouses. The orchestra was ordered to play for the work details in and out of camp morning and evening, tramping past in their rows of five to the sounds of Strauss and Offenbach.

In Raisko the return to some small semblance of normality and physical health had brought with it a need to talk and to exchange stories, always taking care to avoid intimate and painful memories. 'We never spoke', Charlotte would later say, 'of love.' They talked about what they would do after the war, spinning dreams that made them feel they might just still go home. Best was anything to do with literature or the theatre and when Claudette Bloch, Marie-Elisa's chemist friend, revealed that she knew Molière's *Le Malade imaginaire* almost by heart, the Frenchwomen set about recreating the play, line by line, the memories coming back in fits and starts, scene by scene, with Charlotte directing and Cécile once again, as in Romainville, doing the costumes. Cécile had a sharp tongue, but she made the others laugh. Carmen found props; Lulu, who loved acting, took the part of Argan. Aprons were turned into the doctor's gown; tulle netting was borrowed from the laboratory for ruffles, and wood shavings were made into a wig. In the evenings, for an hour at the end of the day, the women rehearsed.

Then came the Sunday of the performance, attended by the whole block. 'It was magnificent,' Charlotte would write, 'because, for the space of two hours, while the smokestacks never stopped belching their smoke of human flesh, for two whole hours we believed in what we were doing.' After remaining silent for so long, the characters of plays and books had finally re-entered Charlotte's mind, and she entertained the others by describing them. Later she would say that she looked in vain for Madame Bovary, Anna Karenina and Rastignac, but that Proust returned to her instead.

On Christmas Eve, the women were permitted to stop work at four. Plans had been made for a dinner of celebration: women celebrating the simple fact that they were not dead, despite all the odds. Their hair had grown back a bit and they helped each other to wash it and brush the new tufts and strands that covered their heads. A few of the women had acquired stockings from 'Canada', and shirts had been 'organized' and cut up to make a clean white collar for each of them. With sheets as tablecloths, the refectory tables were formed into a horseshoe and decorated. Paper was crinkled into flowers, and the chemists had fashioned rouge and lipstick out of powders in the laboratory. Food, saved from the few parcels that were now being allowed in from France, and vegetables pilfered from the gardens were made into a feast of beans and cabbage, potatoes with onion sauce and poppy seeds. The women ate little, having lost the habit of food, but the sight of so much made them cheerful. They drank sweet dark beer, stolen from the SS kitchens. After they had eaten, they turned out the lights, lit candles, and the Polish women with whom the Frenchwomen shared their barracks sang hymns and ballads, saying to each other *Do domou*: back home. Presents were exchanged: a bar of soap; a rope woven into a belt; a teddy bear found near the gas chambers and exchanged for two onions.

Early in the new year an SS guard appeared at Raisko with a list of names. On it were those of most of the Frenchwomen, who were to return immediately to Birkenau. Extremely apprehensive, fearing that an order might have come to kill off the French prisoners, they each packed a small cloth bag and included in it a precious toothbrush and some soap. As they left the barracks, they began to sing the Marseillaise, which had marked every step of their journey. Loaded on to a cart, they went on singing, led by Carmen, who knew a large repertoire of songs. When they saw the barbed wire and the smoking chimney stacks their hearts seemed to stop.

But the news was, as far as they could tell, good. A first party of Frenchwomen was to leave for the camp of Ravensbrück, north of Berlin. Charlotte, Cécile, Poupette, Mado, Lulu, Carmen, Gilberte and Marie-Jeanne were told to undress while slightly cleaner clothes were found for them. Then, to their amazement, their original suitcases, with at least some of their possessions still inside, were returned to them, and they were asked to sign a form swearing not to describe what they had witnessed at Auschwitz. More surprising still,

Rapportführer Taube, whose brutality had coloured many of their days, knelt down to fix Carmen's laces. As if in a dream, they were marched to the station, in their loose striped dresses and ill-fitting shoes, and put on to an ordinary train, where they looked out of the windows at ordinary people going about their lives as if Auschwitz had never existed. They noted with pleasure the degree of damage inflicted by Allied bombing on German towns. The train passed a column of tanks, a Panzer division heading for the Eastern front. What surprised the women most was that they felt so little surprise at the luxury of their surroundings; like coats, left hanging behind a door, they had found their old selves, and it was as if they had never been away.

When they changed trains in Berlin, they found the city in ruins and felt 'nothing but pleasure'. The guards allowed them to go to the women's restrooms and there, for the first time in over a year, they saw themselves in a mirror. They stared with disbelief at their bony, haggard faces and straggling wisps of hair. They discussed trying to escape, but in their distinctive striped clothes they felt there was little chance of success. And where would they have gone? They were herded on to a second train full of Gestapo officers in soft leather coats. Charlotte was touched and amazed when a young woman sitting with her little girl in their compartment insisted that the Frenchwomen take their places. It gave them a sense that there was still a world in which decency and pity existed.

The remaining Frenchwomen remained in their quarantine block outside the fence of Birkenau when Hoess was reappointed commandant, in order to expedite the extermination of the Hungarian Jews, who from May 1944 arrived in the tens of thousands every day. There was now a new railway spur inside Birkenau itself, which led directly to the gas ovens. This meant that there was an assembly line of death, on a scale and at a speed never seen before. One night, Marie-Claude heard terrible cries; next morning she learned that because the gas ovens had run out of Zyklon B pellets, the smaller children had been thrown directly on to the flames. 'When we tell people,' she said to the others, 'who will believe us?'

They were there when the Gypsy family camp was finally cleared. All the small children who had miraculously survived starvation were herded into the gas ovens with their parents. The Frenchwomen still had no news of their fate when an international commission visited Auschwitz and was effectively bamboozled by the SS about the camp's true intent. After the commissioners left, the women were asked whether they wanted to go to work in Germany but they refused, fearing a trap, and so were sent back inside Birkenau, to a wooden barracks just by the railway spur, where they were put to sewing crosses on to ordinary dresses, for Auschwitz had run out of striped material for the new arrivals. They sewed the crosses very loosely, hoping that the wearer might find the chance to escape. From their block they could watch the endless arrivals of Hungarian Jews, and heart-rending scenes when mothers were torn away from their children.

With summer the gardens of Hoess's house, where his children played with balls on the lawn, were full of roses, and begonias grew in his window boxes. Between the barbed-wire fence and the line of rose bushes lay the path leading to the crematoria, and all day long they could see the endless procession of stretchers carrying the dead to the ovens.

The day finally came when the surviving Frenchwomen too were put on to a train for Ravensbrück. Marie-Claude, Marie-Elisa, Adelaide, Germaine Pican and Simone Sampaix were in the first group, followed a few days later by Germaine Renaudin and Hélène Solomon. They were forced to leave behind one member of the *convoi*, Marie-Jeanne Bauer, who had survived typhus and repeated abscesses but now had such bad conjunctivitis that the SS refused to let her go.

The Frenchwomen were now down to fifty-two. What was extraordinary was not that so many had died, but that so many had survived. ■

Ariadne in Triumph

(Roman sarcophagus, second century CE)

The stories are full of these women – Ariadne's
        only one – who cut all ties
to origin and nurture, to the very stones

        and grasses that have heretofore
spelled *home* and we are meant to understand
        they cannot help themselves: it's

love, their great addiction. The hero
        has other axes to grind.
Or clews to follow, something about the larger

        view, requiring
that he sacrifice the merely private sweetness
        of entanglement. To

which – the larger view – we leave him.
        Ariadne meanwhile, though
abandoned, does better than most. See her here

        riding in triumph with
the god she's got as compensation. Ariadne
        at his back, her arm

and leg akimbo, one would never know
         she'd once been brought
so low. It's all before her now:

        the centaurs with their pipes
and lyre, the maenad mid-propulsion with
         her drum. The noise,

the dance, the will-there-be-sex-after-death
        of it, and Ariadne quite
unmoved. I think she likes the lioness.

        Who, striding
one way, gazes back and, just above her
         shoulder, sees exactly

what she's worth to all these revellers:
        an empty skin
that's worn by way of boasting See

        my prowess, as
her own six swollen teats proclaim
        Behold my fruitfulness.

No cubs in sight. As Ariadne has no
        children, just
the starry crown, which is a cleaner

        sort of lastingness.
The better to capture what they must
        have hoped for who

commissioned the sculptor who chiselled
       the stone designed
to hold the body. When I came

       to the museum for a closer
look, the coffin was angled away from
       the wall: New plinth,

explained the carpenter, and let me see
       inside. Where I
beheld the warmer face of it. The

       stained, unfinished, pock-
marked face of breathable oblivion.
       My good wise friend

who does this for a living – makes
       the body's last lodging his daily
work – has no patience for

       the precepts of provident
use: my smallest portion of earth
       and so forth. Give

the dead their due, he says.
       With which
I'm loath to argue, but

       consider the plaque
on the wall: when Rome
       had not yet given up

her flawed republic, even the rich
        expected to come
to ash. The turn

        to empire favoured
marble tombs. And also, as we've seen,
        required some respite

from the weight of all that
        permanence. Hence
Bacchic celebration, hence

        the woman's
mood. She'd give it all up in a heartbeat
        – that's the point

here – for the one
        whose lapse in memory
she's become.

THE DREADFUL
MUCAMAS

Lydia Davis

They are very rigid, stubborn women from Bolivia. They resist and sabotage whenever possible.

They came with the apartment. They were bargains because of Adela's low IQ. She is a scatterbrain.

In the beginning, I said to them: *I'm very happy that you can stay, and I am sure that we will get along very well.*

This is an example of the problems we are having. It is a typical incident that has just taken place. I needed to cut a piece of thread and could not find my six-inch scissors. I accosted Adela and told her I could not find my scissors. She protested that she had not seen them. I went with her to the kitchen and asked Luisa if she would cut my thread. She asked me why I did not simply bite it off. I said I could not thread my needle if I bit it off. I asked her please to get some scissors and cut it off – now. She told Adela to look for the scissors of *la Señora Brodie*, and I followed her to the study to see where they were kept. She removed them from a box. At the same time I saw a long, untidy piece of twine attached to the box and asked her why she did not trim off the frayed end while she had the scissors. She shouted that it was impossible. The twine might be needed to tie up the box some time. I admit that I laughed. Then I took the scissors from her and cut it off myself. Adela shrieked. Her mother appeared behind her. I laughed again and now they both shrieked. Then they were quiet.

I have told them: *Please, do not make the toast until we ask for breakfast. We do not like very crisp toast the way the English do.*

I have told them: *Every morning, when I ring the bell, please bring us our mineral water immediately. Afterwards, make the toast and at the same time prepare fresh coffee with milk. We prefer 'Franja Blanca' or 'Cinta Azul' coffee from Bonafide.*

I spoke pleasantly to Luisa when she came with the mineral water before breakfast. But when I reminded her about the toast, she broke into a tirade – how could I think she would ever let the toast get cold or hard? But it is almost always cold and hard.

We have told them: *We prefer that you always buy 'Las Tres Niñas' or 'Germa' milk from Kasdorf.*

Adela cannot speak without yelling. I have asked her to speak gently, and to say *señora*, but she never does. They also speak very loudly to each other in the kitchen.

Often, before I have said three words to her, she yells at me: *Sí . . . sí, sí, sí . . . !* and leaves the room. I honestly don't think I can stand it.

I say to her: *Don't interrupt me!* I say: *No me interrumpe!*
    I have asked them: *First listen to what I have to say!*

The problem is not that Adela does not work hard enough. But she comes to my room with a message from her mother: she tells me the meal I have asked for is impossible, and she shakes her finger back and forth, screaming at the top of her voice.

They are both, mother and daughter, such wilful, brutal women. At times I think they are complete barbarians.

I have told her: *If necessary, clean the hall, but do not use the vacuum cleaner more than twice a week.*
    Last week she refused point-blank to take the vacuum cleaner out of the front hall by the entrance. Just when we were expecting a visit

from the Rector of Patagonia!

I have asked her: *Please, do not leave the dirt and the cleaning things in the hall.*

I have asked her: *Please, collect the trash and take it to the incinerator immediately.*

They have such a sense of privilege and ownership.

I took my underthings out to them to be washed. Luisa immediately said that it was too hard to wash a girdle by hand. I disagreed, but I did not argue.

When I go to them to enquire about the tasks I have given them, I find they are usually engaged on their own occupations – washing their sweaters or telephoning.

The ironing is never done on time.

Adela refuses to do any work in the mornings but house-cleaning.

I say to them: *We are a small family. We do not have any children.*

Today I reminded them both that my underthings needed to be washed. They did not respond. Finally I had to wash my slip myself.

I say to them: *We have noticed that you have tried to improve, and in particular that you are doing our washing more quickly now.*

Today I said I needed her there in the kitchen, but she went to her mother's room, and came back with her sweater on, and went out anyway. She was buying some lettuce – for them, it turned out, not for us.

At each meal, she makes an effort to escape.

As I was passing through the dining room this morning I tried, as usual, to chat pleasantly with Adela. Before I could say two words, however, she retorted sharply that she could not talk while she was setting the table.

Adela rushes out of the kitchen even when guests are present and shouts: *Telephone for you in your room!*
 Although I have asked her to speak gently, she never does. Today she came rushing in again saying: *Telephone, for you!* and pointed at me. Later she did the same with our luncheon guest, a professor.

I say to Luisa: *I would like to discuss the programme for the days to come. Today I do not need more than a sandwich at noon, and fruit. But* el señor *would like a nutritious tea.*
 Tomorrow we would like a rather nourishing tea with hard-boiled eggs and sardines at six, and we will not want any other meal at home.
 At least once a day, we want to eat cooked vegetables. We like salads, but we also like cooked vegetables. Sometimes we could eat both salad and cooked vegetables at the same meal.
 We do not have to eat meat at lunchtime, except on special occasions. We are very fond of omelettes, perhaps with cheese or tomato.
 Please serve our baked potatoes immediately after taking them from the oven.

We had had nothing but fruit at the end of the meal for two weeks. I asked Luisa for a dessert. She brought me some little crêpes filled with apple sauce. They were nice, though quite cold. Today she gave us fruit again.

I said to her: *Luisa, you cannot refer to my instructions as 'illogical'.*

Luisa is emotional and primitive. Her moods change rapidly. She readily feels insulted and can be violent. She has such pride.
 Adela is simply wild and rough, a hare-brained savage.

I say to Luisa: *Our guest, Señor Flanders, has never visited the park. He would like to spend several hours there. Can you make sandwiches of cold meat for him to take with him? It is his last Sunday here.*

For once, she does not protest.

I say: *Please, I would like Adela to polish the candlesticks. We are going to have them on the table at night.*

When setting the dining table, Adela puts each thing down with a bang.

I ring the bell at the dining table, and a loud crash follows instantly in the kitchen.

I have told them: *There should not be these kitchen noises during our cocktail and dinner hour.*

Luisa, I say, *I want to make sure we understand each other. You cannot play the radio in the kitchen during our dinnertime. There is also a lot of shouting in the kitchen. We are asking for some peace in the house.*

But they are hitting each other again and yelling.

If we ask for something during a meal, she comes out of the kitchen and says: *There isn't any.*

It is all so very nerve-racking. I often feel worn out after just one attempt to speak to her.

We do not believe they are sincerely trying to please us.

Adela sometimes takes the bell off the dining table and does not put it back. Then, I cannot ring for her during the meal, but have to call loudly from the dining room to the kitchen, or go without what I need, or get the bell myself so that I can ring it. My question is: does she leave the bell off the table on purpose?

I instruct them ahead of time: *For the party we will need tomato juice, orange juice and Coca-Cola.*

I tell her: *Adela, you will be the one in charge of answering the door and taking the coats. You will show the ladies where the toilet is, if they ask you.*

I ask Luisa: *Do you know how to prepare* empañadas *in the Bolivian style?*

We would like them both to wear uniforms all the time.

I say to Adela: *Please, I would like you to pass among the guests frequently with plates of hors d'oeuvres that have been recently prepared.*
    When the plates no longer look attractive, please take them back out to the kitchen and prepare fresh ones.

I say to her: *Please, Adela, I would like there always to be clean glasses on the table, and also ice and soda.*

I have told her: *Always leave a towel on the rack above the bidet.*

I say to her: *Are there enough vases? Can you show them to me? I would like to buy some flowers.*

I see that Adela has left a long string lying on the floor next to the bed. She has gone away with the waste basket. I don't know if she is testing me. Does she think I am too meek or ignorant to require her to pick it up? But she has a cold, and she isn't very bright, and if she really did not notice the string, I don't want to make too much of it. I finally decide to pick up the string myself.

We suffer from their rude and ruthless vengeance.

A button was missing from my husband's shirt collar. I took the shirt to Adela. She shook her finger and said no. She said that *la Señora*

Brodie always took everything to the dressmaker to be mended.
Even a button? I asked. Were there no buttons in the house?
She said there were no buttons in the house.

I told Luisa they could go out on Sundays, even before breakfast. She yelled at me that they did not want to go out, and asked me, where would they go?

I said that they were welcome to go out, but that if they did not go out, we would expect them to serve us something, even if it was something simple. She said she would, in the morning, but not in the afternoon. She said that her two older daughters always came to see her on Sundays.

I spent the morning writing Luisa a long letter, but I decided not to give it to her.

In the letter I told Luisa: *I have employed many maids in my life.*

I told her that I believe I am a considerate, generous and fair employer.

I told her that when she accepts the realities of the situation, I'm sure everything will go well.

If only they would make a real change in their attitude, we would like to help them. We would pay to have Adela's teeth repaired, for instance. She is so ashamed of her teeth.

But up to now there has been no real change in their attitude.

We also think they may have relatives living secretly with them behind the kitchen.

I am learning and practising a sentence that I will try on Luisa, though it may sound more hopeful than I feel: *Con el correr del tiempo, todo se solucionará.*

But they give us such dark, Indian looks! ■

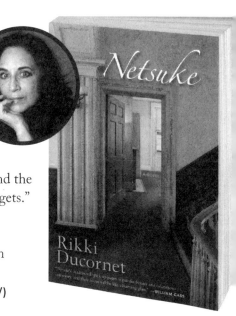

A KEPT WOMAN

Laura Bell

Years ago when I applied for a job with the Bighorn National Forest in Wyoming, I wrote a cover letter that focused on all the things I knew I could do alone in a remote environment: haul, ride and pack horses; build and fix a fence; operate heavy equipment; run vegetative surveys; find my way around the backcountry wilderness. The office manager who was coaching me lifted an eyebrow and said, 'But Laura, they don't really want to know all the things you can do by yourself. They want to know that you can work with others. That you can be a *team player*.'

The concept had never occurred to me. I thought that the ultimate accomplishment was to be able to 'do it by myself'.

Most of my life I've scrambled to do just that. At twenty-three, I moved to Wyoming and for three years herded a band of a thousand sheep out on its northern high-desert ranges, six months at a stretch. There were no hot showers, and it was long before the days of cellphones and the Internet. Surrounded by miles of sagebrush and days defined by weather, I packed a rifle, read books and cared for the dogs and horse that became my family. I was a young woman in a male world of eccentrics, alcoholics and hermits. I didn't complain; I loved it. I chose it.

From sheep camp, I moved on to cowboy for a family ranch in Shell Valley, to managing livestock grazing on the Bighorn Forest, to practising massage, to running horse-pack trips in the backcountry of Yellowstone, to overseeing conservation projects and fund-raising for the Wyoming Nature Conservancy. My résumé may be a hodgepodge of experience, but in thirty-five years of adult life, I have never been without a pay cheque, never depended on another's to pay my rent or mortgage.

After my first book, a memoir, was published last spring, my partner was offered a lucrative job outside our home state and proposed that 'we' take it. 'It's plenty enough for both of us, and you could write full-time. We could keep the Cody house so we always have a Wyoming home. Would you come with me?'

Six months later, I'm surprised at what an easy decision that was for me, who has never in my life followed anyone anywhere. Ever. 'I'll be a kept woman,' I'd say to my friends, tongue in cheek, though I had ambitious plans for a next book and a hard-wired work ethic. After many years of carrying the wage-earning ball, I revelled at the prospect of time to read and write, to research my next project. What I didn't realize was how much I would also love having the time to make a home, to figure out how things work and how to fix them. I accept that, to some degree, this big job belongs to both of us, and I've picked up the slack of doing housework and running errands. I've been the one to fix breakfast every morning, pack him lunch and, at day's end, spread out wine and cheese and olives to welcome him home. In the hours between, I retire with my books, laptop and dogs to the backyard, to the little Airstream that serves as my writing studio.

And yet, in those hours when the words won't come, when I long to the point of tears for the horizon of mountains we left behind, I falter. It's what I'd said I wanted – time to write – but nothing like how I imagined it would be, separated for much of the year from the western landscape, history and community that have sustained me the last thirty years.

The question was asked of me by the man that I love, a man that I trust and respect. 'Will you come with me?' And for the first time in my life I simply said 'yes' and walked into this unknown country, a few backward glances over my shoulder to make sure the doors weren't clanging shut behind me.

Now I find myself walking the high trail between fear and love, wavering in my path. When I stumble to my deepest fear, I imagine that my choices have rendered me powerless, that I've become the 'kept woman' of my banter.

I am sure, now, of my substance in a way that I never was at twenty or thirty or forty. Except in my lowest moments, I no longer measure my worth by the dollars I produce. But after the unpacking and settling in, the initial excitement of what we've called 'a sabbatical' and my joy at the empty time to write, I feel a loss that I had never imagined. I understand that I left behind the people, the landscape, even the weather that reflects back to me my strongest self. In this transition, I can't be sure that the sentences I'm creating are of value. And there's no one here, except for my husband, who knows me. Sometimes in the solitude of this strange place I forget who I am.

In the mix of these days I know I will make choices, seemingly small and obscure, that can render me powerless or sharpen my blade. It's my job to pay attention. I have a partner and a circle of friends and family, far and wide, who will support me, 'keeping me' in the best sense of those words. ∎

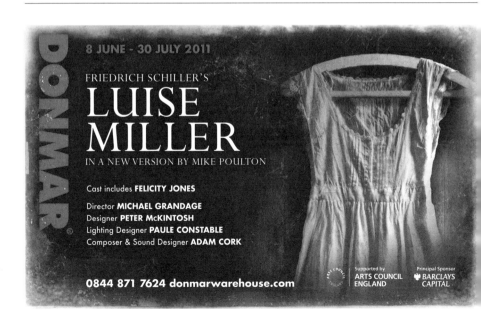

ENJOYING YOURSELF?

Have *Granta* delivered to your door four times a year and save up to 42% on the cover price.

'Still the coolest magazine to have on your coffee table.' – *Observer*

UK
£34.95 (£29.95 Direct Debit)

Europe
£39.95

Rest of the world★
£45.95

Subscribe now by completing the form overleaf, visiting granta.com or calling free phone 0500 004 033

★Not for people in America, Canada or Latin America – there's one of these cards just for you a bit further on…

GRANTA.COM

GRANTA

THE MAGAZINE OF NEW WRITING

SUBSCRIPTION FORM FOR UK, EUROPE AND REST OF THE WORLD

Yes, I would like to take out a subscription to *Granta*.

YOUR DETAILS

MR / MISS / MRS / DR ....

NAME ....

ADDRESS ....

....

POSTCODE ....

EMAIL ....

(Only provide your email if you are happy for Granta to communicate with you this way)

☐ Please tick this box if you do not wish to receive special offers from *Granta*

☐ Please tick this box if you do not wish to receive offers from organizations selected by *Granta*

YOUR PAYMENT DETAILS

1) ☐ Pay £29.95 (saving £22) by Direct Debit
   To pay by Direct Debit please complete the mandate below and return to the address shown above.

2) Pay by cheque or credit/debit card. Please complete below:

   1 year subscription: ☐ UK: £34.95   ☐ Europe: £39.95   ☐ Rest of World: £45.95

   3 year subscription: ☐ UK: £89.95   ☐ Europe: £99   ☐ Rest of World: £122

   I wish to pay by   ☐ CHEQUE   ☐ CREDIT/DEBIT CARD
   Cheque enclosed for £ —————— made payable to *Granta*.

   Please charge £ —————— to my: ☐ Visa ☐ Mastercard ☐ Amex ☐ Switch/Maestro ☐ Issue No
   Card No. ☐☐☐☐☐☐☐☐☐☐☐☐☐☐☐☐☐

   Valid from *(if applicable)* ☐☐☐☐   Expiry Date ☐☐☐☐
   Security No. ☐☐☐

SIGNATURE .... DATE ....

Instructions to your Bank or Building Society to pay by Direct Debit

BANK NAME ....

BANK ADDRESS ....

POSTCODE ....

ACCOUNT IN THE NAMES(S) OF: ....

SIGNED ....

DATE ....

Bank/building society account number
☐☐☐☐☐☐☐☐

Sort Code
☐☐☐☐☐☐

Originator's Identification
9 1 3 1 3 3

Please mail this order form with payment instructions to:

Freepost RSBU-BZZL-KSJG
Granta Publications
12 Addison Avenue
London, W11 4QR
Or call 0500 004 033
or visit GRANTA.COM

THE OJIBWE WEEK

Louise Erdrich

Giziibiigisaginige-giizhigad

Klaus Shawano lives in exactly half of the bottom floor of a duplex built in 1872 and owned now by his friend and boss, Richard Whiteheart Beads. His main room, once the dining room, has a rippled old window topped with a stained-glass panel. Even though the old window looks directly into the window of a brand-new lower-income housing unit built smack on the property line of Andrew Jackson Street, just off Franklin Avenue, an occasional shaft of morning radiance sometimes stirs in the prisms of stained glass. When that happens, bands of coloured light quiver on the mottled walls. The bed, a savage hummocky mattress laid on top of an even older mattress and box spring, which in turn is nailed right into the floor, sometimes catches the rainbows in its gnarled sheets and blankets. The rainbows move across the bodies of late sleepers. Klaus watches the sheaf of colours waver slowly through Sweetheart Calico's hair and then across her brow. The rainbow slides down her face, a shimmering veil. When she wakes up, she doesn't move except to sag with disappointment. Her eyes are dead and sad, killing the rainbow, catching at his heart.

'We are codependent,' he says. 'I read it in a newspaper. We are at risk, you and I. Well, you most of all, since you are the one tied to the bed.'

A curtain tie-back solidly bolted into the wall acts as a hitching post for Sweetheart Calico. A web of makeshift restraints bind her ankles, wrists. There is even a cord around her waist, tied with complicating rosebud cloth and functioning as a sleep sash. Klaus unties her and she rises, naked, yawning. She rubs one ankle with the side of the opposite foot and stretches her arms. She floats to the bathroom breathing an old tune – she doesn't talk to Klaus but she's always whispering songs much older and stranger than any powwow or sweat lodge or even sun-dance song he has ever heard. There are flushing sounds, water, a shower. She loves the shower and will stand beneath it smiling for half an hour and would stay longer if Rozin, wife of Richard Whiteheart Beads and monitor of hot-water use in this joint living space, didn't stop her.

'I need some hot water for cleaning,' she calls down the stairs.

Giziibiigisaginige-giizhigad is the Ojibwe word for Saturday and means floor-washing day. Which tells you that nobody cared what day of the week it was until the Ojibwe had floors and also that the Ojibwe wash their floors.

We are a clean people, Klaus thinks. He knocks on the bathroom door. He opens the door and when he sees the bathroom window is wide open, in spite of the child-safety locks he installed, he knows without looking behind the shower curtain that she is gone.

Anama'e-giizhigad

Although the Ojibwe never had a special day to pray until mission and boarding schools taught how you could slack off the rest of the week, this day now has its name. Praying Day. Klaus spent all day yesterday walking the streets and bushwhacking down by the river and questioning. Questioning people.

'Have you seen a naked beautiful Indian woman hanging around here by any chance? Or she could be wearing just a towel?'

'Bug off, asshole.'

'She's mine,' he says. 'Don't touch her.'

Yesterday he walked a hundred miles. At least he felt like it. Today, on Praying Day, he takes out the pipe that his father was given when he returned home safe from the war.

'I'll be asking the Creator for some assistance,' he says to his father's pipe as he fits it together and loads it while singing the song that goes along with loading a pipe. He takes from a slip of cardboard a feather that he uses to fan the ember at the heart of a small wad of sage. The smoke rises and rolls. He has disabled the smoke alarm.

'I pledge this feather to my woman if she returns of her own free will,' he says between smokes.

The feather is very special, a thunderbird feather. A long pure white one that dropped one day out of an empty sky.

Dropped into my life just like you, my darling, sweetgrass love, Klaus thinks. The smoke curls comfortingly around his head. But he smokes his pipe too much. He smokes it again and again until his head aches and his chest is clogged. He will cough for the rest of the day and every time he does a puff of smoke will pop from his lungs.

Dizzy, he breaks down his pipe, cleans it, puts it carefully away. He rolls the pipestone bowl in his father's sock – all, besides the pipe and his deaf ear, that he's got left from his father. Unless you count his libido. And, of course, his lips.

'You got a lip line a girl would kill for,' one of his not-girlfriends had said to him. Those plush yet sculpted lips were his father's lips. Many times they fit around this pipe stem, this *okij*. Klaus rolls that in a red-and-white buckshot bag. He puts the feather back into its fold of cardboard and stashes these sacred items on the highest shelf of the kitchen cabinet. He feels much better. He goes out to talk with Richard Whiteheart Beads. He coughs. A puff of smoke.

'Is that a smoke signal?' Richard says. 'What are you trying to tell me?'

'Have you seen a beautiful naked antelope lady running through the streets?'

'She escaped? That's good. You can't just keep a woman tied up in your room, you know. Rozin suspects. If she finds out she'll get in touch with the women's crisis hotline. I don't want the police coming around here. Plus, my girls. What kind of example for them?'

Klaus coughs.

'Oh, I got that signal,' Richard says. 'Me fucked.'

'That is the problem,' says Klaus. 'She has enslaved me with her antelope ways.'

'You one sad mess,' says Richard. 'Let her go.'

But Klaus goes out into the night and continues to search the streets of the night of Praying Day, which are quiet and peaceful and empty.

Nitam-anokii-giizhigad

First Work Day. Proving that the names of the days of the week are the products of colonized minds. What a name for Monday. Rubbing it in that work starts early in the a.m. with Richard. Today they are ripping carpet out of the soon to be renovated Prairiewood Rivertree Mall next to the Foreststream Manor.

Carpets in malls are always the colour of filth. In the petrochemical nap the hue of every excrescence from shit to trodden vomit comes up beneath their prying and ripping tools. They carry roll after roll of the stuff out to Richard's fancy yellow pickup truck. Even Klaus thinks it's way too visible. They are being paid to dispose of a toxic substance and Richard has the perfect place.

Land chequerboard was one gift of the Dawes or General Allotment Act of 1887 that otherwise dispossessed Klaus and Richard's forefathers of 90 per cent of the Indian Lands that were left after the red-hot smoke of treaty signing. The chequerboard. The reservation, which they drive to from the city, is a chequerboard – white squares and red squares – denoting ownership. On one white square a big farm stands, owned by a retired Norwegian couple who winter and sometimes spring and even fall in Florida. Richard has rented their farm under an assumed name. He and Klaus are now quickly filling the barn with carpet, which costs a pretty penny to dispose of in an EPA-designated hazardous waste site or costs nothing to put in a barn.

'They won't mind. They won't even notice. They never go out to the barn.'

'You sure?' asks Klaus on *Nitam-anokii-giizhigad*. They are unloading the ripped-up carpet. Roll after noxious roll. The rolls are bound with the same cord hanging from the hitching post next to Klaus's bed. Klaus and Richard have made meticulously neat stacks, filling the cow stalls level. They make certain that each layer is completely solid, packing in the gaps between rows with carpet scraps.

We are doing a bad thing, but we are doing it well, thinks Klaus.

For his part, Richard uses compartmentalization. Its extreme usefulness cannot be overestimated. Richard first learned of the term from Rozin. He was surprised to find there was a word for what he was already doing to accommodate the knockings of his conscience.

On some level, he says to his conscience, this is certainly wrong. Not only will the old couple be stuck with hazardous waste, but the chequerboard is reservation board and thus eligible for tribal homeland status if the casino ever turns a profit, as it may never do, being poorly managed, but theoretically there might be enough money in the tribal coffers one day to repurchase this old farm and add it to tribal trust lands. Only first there'd be the problem of disposing of as many tons of carpet as this barn will hold and it looks like it will hold an awful lot.

Wall. Wall. Wall. Compartment.

Meanwhile, Richard is pocketing the money paid him to dispose properly of righteous poisons. Some of it he pays to Klaus.

Even if this land is owned by Norwegians it is still Mother Earth, thinks Klaus. *Nookomis*, please forgive me. I am sorry. I am doing a very tidy job of hurting you, if that makes a difference.

He takes his gloves off and says that a beer would go down good.

'Let's hit a bar on the way home,' says Richard. And so they do. And they are finished with *Nitam-anokii-giizhigad*.

Niizho-giizhigad

Life is hell without her tied up next to me. Klaus mourns all night and dismally wakes on the Second Day. A Work Day. All the Ojibwe do is work, you would think. Work and pray. Again the carpet-ripping and the fetid stink of concrete underneath and again the thoughtful cerebral work of stacking in the barn. Stacking for the future so that the two can climb on to the neat floor from the stairs up to the hayloft and not die in a carpet quake or be swallowed up in a carpet-roll crevasse.

Sweetheart Calico, Sweetheart Calico. My bitter black heart is bursting open, Klaus whispers. His chest still hurts from the intense smoke-praying that he did two days ago and from all the secular inhalations in the days since. There's been no clue, no lead, no sighting of the woman he kidnapped – no, she went willingly. Didn't she? It's all unclear. He put her in his van at the powwow and took her home and got addicted to her.

Your sex love should be declared a controlled substance, he thinks now. I am experiencing severe withdrawal. He shakes as he stuffs ripped carpet down the seams of the next layer of carpet-roll floor. He should not have done what he did – stolen her, gotten her drunk, loved her, tied her up. Except she asked for it with her eyes. Which Rozin will tell him should get him ten to twenty years in Stillwater.

'She never asked for nothing with her eyes, you criminal,' Rozin says that evening when he weeps at her kitchen table. 'Except for you to let her go. You compartmentalized. You put your mental processes in only part of your brain so you can enjoy yourself. Even when what you are doing is a crime.'

'But she tied me up, too,' says Klaus. 'She tied me up with those same ropes.'

'And left you there, right?'

'Yes,' says Klaus in a small voice. 'I thought something else was going to happen that time. She came back though of her own free will because she loves me.'

'She came back because she has nowhere to go. Where did you steal her from? Where are her people?'

'They are nomadic.'

'Tell that to the cops.'

'They roam Montana,' says Klaus.

Out where the barns are filled with hay, not carpet. Though he knows from the great rolls of carpet glued to the floors of acres of malls all through Montana that this is not true and conceivably there could even be two Indians like Klaus and Richard out there disposing of old carpet on their own federal trust land where special rules apply.

Aabitoose

Halfway. How is it that with all the names for the months and seasons and the lyrical possibilities in the origins of this most extraordinary language the best that can be done for Wednesday is Halfway? To where? To the end of the week or to the day of fun when we wash the floors? *Aabitoose* is the day Rozin goes to the bakery owned by Frank Shawano, a relative of Klaus. Frank's Bakery is a real old-fashioned, independent little bakery like the kind there used to be, with hand-fried doughnuts – not donuts, the 'ugh' makes them Indian and heavier. Rozin goes to the bakery after the girls are on the school bus because she needs a coffee lift before her job. She is a supermarket checker. There is also Frank himself, an old friend with a crush on her. She likes pretending that his flirting annoys her. She doesn't go because she wants to find Klaus's girlfriend whom he claims in his emotional confusion is part antelope.

But there she is. A dog lolling next to her.

Sweetheart Calico and the dog sit side by side on the kerb just outside the shop. A car could run right over Sweetheart's tiny feet. The dog is grey, shaggy like a coyote. Sweetheart Calico is arrestingly graceful, but tired. She is a tired, tired woman with tangled hair, wearing a huge pair of jeans belonging to Klaus Shawano and a shirt that could belong to anybody in the neighbourhood as it is a huge black T-shirt with an airbrushed buffalo stampeding away from an American flag and through a hoop of fire with an eagle screaming at its shoulder and beneath its hooves a wolf and bear also running for their lives and all of the animals surrounded by thunder and lightning. You see that exact T-shirt on every other person on the street but this particular shirt belongs to Klaus.

'Oh my God. Here you are. Are you all right, Sweetheart? Come and have a coffee with me.'

Sweetheart Calico holds in her hands a tawny, fragrant, puffed-up ball of dough with a saddle of lemon jelly that quivers when she takes a bite. She throws half the pastry to the dog, who snarfs it mid-air. Mouth full, she follows Rozin into the bakery where there are three tables with two chairs each that fit right against the window. Frank has a Bunn coffee-maker – just decent old-fashioned coffee – one dollar a large mug or free with any pastry.

'You forgot your free coffee,' he says now to Sweetheart Calico, though he gave her the pastry too, free, and now gives her another lemon-jelly doughnut.

The dog waits, alert, right outside the door. Frank just smiles at Rozin, because all of the awkward, semi-suggestive lines about fresh buns and long johns were used up long ago.

'*Niinimoshenh*, what can I get for you?'

Rozin ignores that word which means my sweetheart but which also used to mean my sex-eligible cousin. She examines the trays of chocolate eclairs, bismarcks, maple logs – no scones or lumpy vegan muffins here. She buys a cup of coffee and selects a loaf of bread. Gives it to Frank for slicing.

Rozin and Sweetheart Calico sit down with their coffees at a table in the sun of the window.

'Are you OK? Why did you run away from Klaus? Is that sucker mean to you?'

Sweetheart Calico shrugs and licks sugar off her fingers. *I am lost,* her look says. *I don't know how I got here.*

She stuffs the jelly doughnut into her mouth. The lemon filling has real lemon in it, sweet and tart.

'Do you want to come home with me? I'll let you in downstairs. You can sleep. You can shower.'

Sweetheart Calico glances out of the window at the dog. Rozin makes a face. 'OK it can come too.'

Frank gathers the slices from the machine into a tight transparent bag. He walks over to them, holding out the loaf, so fresh it sags between his hands like an accordion.

Halfway Day. If it was All The Way Day things might have gone much differently. But Rozin only walks halfway inside of the downstairs apartment. The dog, too; halfway in. Then it settles on the floor. Sweetheart Calico is halfway glad to get home. The twins, Cally and Deanna, do halfway well at school and make it halfway home on the bus before they sort of fight and pretty much make up. Rozin halfway wants to quit work as usual, but does not. Klaus and Richard work hard and the barn is half full when they leave. Unfortunately, at home the meat is halfway cooked because the electricity has gone out and the crockpot is cold when Rozin touches it. Then Richard and Klaus are cleaning up at the same time and you can hear them yell halfway through their showers when cold water hits their skin.

Later, Rozin is halfway through sex with Richard when she thinks of Frank Shawano holding that bread. She tries to push the picture out of her mind. What's he doing there? Get away, she thinks. No, come back. The picture makes her feel something she was not feeling before. Richard has been drinking with Klaus after work but he is not even halfway drunk. He has been patient about the half-cooked meat. He has listened with half an ear to all that his daughters did during the day. So Rozin should be at least halfway into sex, which is all it really takes to satisfy Richard. But she isn't. She is somewhere else. Afterwards she turns away with the sudden feeling that her heart is breaking right in . . . not half – it is shattering into golden infinitesimal fragments. It is bursting and the grains are flying fast against the sun. Her heart is pollen glinting on the wind. No, it is flour, blowing toward Frank's bakeshop wanting to get mixed in his batter with eggs and sugar and formed into a doughnut. Her heart travels faster and faster, toward Frank's deep-fryer, and all the time Richard thinks she is asleep, weighted firmly in the dark that will become tomorrow.

Niiyo-giizhigad

Pragmatical disappointment! Day Four. And so many other choices for this poetic day – a day near the freedom of the weekend yet not the frantic rush to get your work done, not yet. A day that can almost stand by itself because of its special ceremonial associations in Ojibwe teachings. Anyway, Day Four. Day of new existence. Day of anything can happen. Day of pollen on the wind. Day of Klaus half awake tied to his own bed by Sweetheart Calico and thinking in his dream that he hears the clatter of her hooves as she runs wildly back and forth bashing into unfamiliar walls and believing that when he opens his eyes his sheets will be covered with her inky cloven erotic tracks.

Actually, she is outside playing with her new dog. Well, not new. That dog is definitely second-hand, thinks Klaus. It is a used dog, a thrift-store dog, at best a dollar-store animal with its skinny legs, big belly, scraggy, pedigreeless fur. And its head is way big for the rest of it, like a sample fur toy that was never produced en masse but thrown into a discount bin.

I don't like that dog, he thinks. There is definitely something sinister about its big, round, grinning head.

And it growled when he took the rope out last night.

Forget about locking me in the bathroom, its look said, I'll shit on the floor.

Then it growled worse and worse until he handed the rope to Sweetheart Calico.

At least Day Four is about four, the number that the Ojibwe love best of all. Every good and sustaining thing comes in fours – seasons, directions, types of people, medicines, elements. There are four layers of the earth, four layers of the sky, four push-ups to a song, four honour beats, four pauses of the great Megis on the spiritual migration to Gakahbekong and hereabouts. So why shouldn't today, which partakes of that exquisite number, be an extremely lucky day, thinks Klaus, although I can feel the cords that bind my wrists and ankles tightly and I remember somewhere in the night that she wrapped her long tense legs around my body and used special antelope knots on me.

'Oh no.' Klaus speaks but doesn't open his eyes. He whispers. 'Are you there?'

Day Four began so well for Cally and Deanna. Instead of iron-fortified and vitamin-enriched sugarless multigrain cereal flakes, instead of the stinky-boy cackling bus, their mom takes them to the bakery for anything they want and drives them to school in her car. And says, glowing happily, 'Girls, we should do this more often!'

Blood sugar peaking from the cracked glaze on the doughnuts and the eclair custard, both of them swear thrillingly that they will become A+ not B- students if this regimen is followed by their mother. Rozin laughs. They stand on the sidewalk in front of the bank of school entryway doors, waving until her car is down the street.

They look at each other and both say at once, 'Is Mom OK?' Then they say in unison, 'Get out of my head.' They scream with laughter and walk to the doors, doubled over. When the sugar wears off and smacks them to the harsh floor of the gym at 9 a.m. and they profess to be ill, both are sent to the school nurse who takes their temperatures with fever strips and gives them each a plastic cup of high fructose-enhanced orange juice. Jacked up for another few hours, they return to class and do a prodigious pile of pre-algebra equations, which they both love. An affinity for numbers! They were born on the fourth day of the fourth month at 4.00 and 4.04. So no wonder they are not to be mistaken for ordinary twins at all. They are mystic twins, like the twins who created the world. Only, those first twins inarguably fucked it up and if Cally and Deanna had a chance they would make the world properly. In fact, they make the world up all of the time. It is their favourite thing to do when they get home from school.

Cally and Deanna start to draw the world after school on *Niiyo-giizhigad*, but a dog brought home by Sweetheart Calico interrupts. It barks as it chases Sweetheart Calico around and around the weedy yard. The antelope woman laughs silently as she leaps on high heels evading its teeth and paws. The dog jumps and twists in the air looking like a big grey wind-tossed rag. It isn't a very good-looking dog. Couldn't be called any one particular breed of dog. Yet a sympathy for humans shines out of its eyes and the girls fall instantly in love, not knowing that this very dog is the fourth dog of the fourth litter of the forty-fourth daughter of the dog named Sorrow.

They join in running and playing tag with the dog and with the woman whose great-great-grandmother on her human side slit the throat of that ancestor dog and boiled its meat so that her daughter would have the strength to travel into the blue west, wearing the same blue beads that Sweetheart Calico hides now as she leaps away from the dog, laughing that wild and silent laugh. She screams noiselessly, even as poor Klaus, whom she has freed to go to work that morning, creeps into the apartment and showers off the greasy grit of random Minneapolis citizens whose shoes mashed every form of personal grunge into the mall carpeting and transferred that human scurf to Klaus so that he's covered utterly with the invisible populace – including refugees from every danger zone in the universe. And it won't wash away. Twin-cities people have entered his very pores and he has breathed them in also so that he is now inhabited by the world's thousands. Dead and living. Brand new and ancient. Bargain-hunting ghosts inhabit Klaus on Day Four of the week as Rozin too returns from her work and says, *what the hell is going on in this madhouse*, but wearily smiles as her daughters are whirling and chasing and full of life and if Rozin half closes her eyes and watches them through the blur of eyelashes she sees the unutterable grace of antelope children galloping mid-air.

Naano-giizhigad

Day Five. There are so many other good names for this almost-there day when you wake and think *tomorrow I can sleep*. The morning will bring the rainbows on again like last week and Klaus can watch them cross the elegant wild structure of her face. Tomorrow, for Cally and Deanna, there will be drawing and a dog to play with and no more teacher's dirty looks or locker-slamming-on-your-fingers boys who suck dead rats and pretend that Cally and Deanna are Chinese or Hmong or Mexican and sneer *go back where you came from.*

'That's just boys,' says Rozin. 'Go back where you came from! How can you say that to a Native Person?'

'I'll fix 'em. I'll go right in there,' says Richard.

But here it is, Day Five, and he and Klaus must pull up the last of the carpet.

'Go then,' says Rozin.

The girls watch for a kiss between them but are disappointed. They have noticed that their mother likes to talk to Frank Shawano and their father's eyes follow Sweetheart Calico even though she is Klaus's girlfriend. And all of these grown-up doings make them sick, sick, sick. They'd rather make the world over in girl image. The world would be only girls and animals and no boys or disappointing grownups except perhaps their mother visits bringing favourite food once every two weeks and long hugs but I could last a month, says Cally.

'Nobody mean can live on our planet,' says Deanna.

'And the dog will be our brother.'

'We won't take husbands.'

'Obviously.'

Why can't this be the day of the otter, the kingfisher, the coot, the loon, the balsam tree, the moccasin flower or the trout? The Ojibwe words for all of these lovely animals and plants are original and fluid words but in all probability some lacklustre hard-assed missionary Jesuit like maybe Bishop Baraga the famous Snowshoe Priest put those names down in his Ojibwe dictionary in the hope of making the Ojibwe people into hard-ass lacklustre people like him by forcing them to live every day of their lives working or praying or halfway to nowhere. Many days of the week in English go back to various ancient pagan gods (Thor's day, Frieda's day, Saturn's day . . .). *Naano-giizhigad* would be so much better as *Nanabozhoo-giizhigad* as *Nanabozhoo* was a great teacher who taught lessons through foul hilarity and amoral idiocy, so the day could celebrate and commemorate the great lessons learned from fools like Klaus.

For he knows he is a major doof to work for Richard on this scam, which becomes every day more deadly and strange as the carpet mounts in the barn and the cheques get written out and Richard signs his name on government paperwork.

'That's *government* paperwork,' Klaus notices.

Richard winks a movie-star wink, an old-time black-and-white-movie lip-hanging-cigarette wink. Thank God it's *Naano-giizhigad* and they can get the hell out of the barn before the ghost carpet swallows them.

'It's all over, my friend,' says Richard. 'Let us cash these obscenely fat cheques and treat our wives to a fancy dinner.'

'My lady don't sit still,' says Klaus. 'She likes to take long walks. We buy food on the way. We keep walking.'

'C'mon, say it, Klaus. She likes to graze.'

'Shut up,' says Klaus.

'You should bring her back to where you got her. She's trouble. She's a goddamn ungulate.'

'I know,' says Klaus. 'But I can't let go.'

Neither of them remark on Richard's use of a high-school vocabulary word, which he has carefully saved up until this moment. He has also saved what he thinks is a Zen saying.

'You can hold more water in an open hand than in a closed fist,' says Richard.

'That's ridiculous,' says Klaus. 'You can hold the neck of a bottle in your closed fist.'

'I hadn't thought of that. You're not tying her up any more . . .'

'No, she's got a dog now and it bites.'

'Serves you right.'

'Now she's the one who ties me up.'

'I don't think I'd like that,' says Richard.

'It's pretty good though,' says Klaus. 'Except when she runs away and leaves me there.'

They drive to the divided-up house built ten years after the murderous year in Minnesota when the starving Dakota were told by an Indian Agent that their dying children should eat grass. The house, now inhabited by the Whiteheart Beads and Shawanos and one antelope woman and a dog, was built by a soldier who'd come home from the Civil War with a sickened heart that he could only numb by pounding nail after nail. So it is well built. Klaus and Richard park the car on the beaten-down part of the yard that has become driveway. Cally and Deanna looking out of their window watch them remove a case of beer each from the trunk.

'Let's leave them out of our world,' they say in unison. 'Jinx!'

They slap hands, spin hands, rap their hands up and down and ruffle the air four times to seal in the luck of words spoken together. Rozin walks out of the door and says to Richard, 'Watch the girls. I have to go buy a loaf of bread.' The descendant of Sorrow slides along the foundation to the alley dense with buckthorn and mulberry. The dog ambles close to and settles down by Sweetheart Calico who stands very still in the leaves, believing she is invisible. ■

Iphigenia in Forest Hills: Anatomy of a Murder Trial *Janet Malcolm*

A prize-winning journalist discovers the elements of Greek tragedy in a sensational murder trial. This is a riveting account of the recent bizarre and intriguing Borukhova case. Janet Malcolm's journalistic brilliance paints an unsettling picture of a fractured marriage, legal manoeuvrings and a fatal custody battle that precipitated murder.

Yale University Press £18.00 | HB

Wasafiri

Since the first issue was published in 1984, *Wasafiri* has always opened minds and crossed literary worlds. The magazine remains key in mapping new literary landscapes and offering the best of contemporary international writing, consistently featuring Britain's diverse cultural heritage while also highlighting the vast range of worldwide diasporic and migrant literature. Further details at www.wasafiri.org/subscribe.asp

Wasafiri | Individual subscriptions £44 / €61 / $78

A Book for All and None *Clare Morgan*

Raymond, a brilliant but ageing don, has withdrawn into a lonely world of scholarship. Beatrice is in Oxford researching Virginia Woolf, and distancing herself from her semi-estranged husband, Walter. When Beatrice appears in Raymond's life, they embark on a love affair and uncover a secret that will profoundly change their understanding of who they really are. A tantalizing literary mystery.

Weidenfeld & Nicolson £12.99 | HB

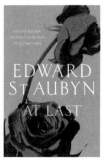

At Last *Edward St Aubyn*

The eagerly anticipated new novel from Man Booker Prize-shortlisted Edward St Aubyn. For Patrick Melrose, 'family' is more than a double-edged sword. As friends, relations and foes trickle in to pay their final respects to his mother, Patrick finds that his transition to orphanhood isn't necessarily the liberation he had so long imagined. A masterpiece of glittering dark comedy and emotional truth. May 2011

Picador.com/atlast

NIGHT THOUGHTS

Helen Simpson

3:29 a.m.

Foolishly he had opened his eyes, and that was the time. Under four hours. He'd never get back. The straight-sided digits floated, gloated, lime green in the dark. That was tomorrow shot. Meanwhile Ella snored on beside him, oblivious.

Within ten seconds he was as wide awake as she was deep asleep. No, they hadn't started out like this but this was life now. What she couldn't seem to understand was that it was hard, he found it very hard to run the house and look after her and the children as well as hold down a full-time job. It surprised him – embarrassed him, even – that she couldn't seem to see this for herself. Didn't she care? If he said anything though she got angry and walked out of the room.

3:32 a.m.

Think about something else. The Performance Management Review coming up at school next week. Another teaching hoop to jump through. His line manager would be observing him formally and every single one of his students would need to be seen as having made exceptional progress during the observed lesson for him to get an Outstanding. He was breaking into a light sweat just thinking about it.

He wanted to go part-time. That was what he was nerving himself up for. Dave Sweetland had agreed to a job-share if they could get it past the Head. Part-time would mean he'd be able to cook something other than pasta and help Colin more with his homework and generally keep an eye on him – he was worried about him – as well as do boring but necessary things like sort out the boiler and take Daisy to the dentist and get his marking done before midnight. It would make all the difference. But he would have to be careful how he approached Ella.

It was so hard. If he got the wrong tone of voice she shouted and refused to listen. It was like treading on eggshells. Feminine pride. He'd have to present it to her as her own idea, that's what he'd have to do. If he could somehow show her that her life too would be improved by it, then it might work.

He cringed now, turning on to his right side, and curled into a foetal position. Whenever he said anything, she started talking about certain men at the hospital where she was Director of Facilities, working fathers who managed to do it all effortlessly and without fuss.

She'd say, Money. But he was going to get ill otherwise.

3:37 a.m.

Stop worrying. Count backwards from a thousand. Nine hundred and ninety-nine. That was another good worry, whether he'd done the right thing not to report what he'd been told at the last school parents' evening. Timothy Tisdall's father had sat opposite him for the obligatory four minutes and with tear-filled eyes had whispered to him what he suffered at the hands of his wife; how his wife was a policewoman so knew not to hit him anywhere it would show; how he couldn't report it and was begging him not to report it but how he had to tell someone and thank you for listening, it made him feel less alone.

There was a bit of pushing and shoving sometimes from Ella, but she didn't hit him. Nine hundred and ninety-eight. Not nice to think how the overwhelming majority of men who were murdered were murdered by their own wives.

3:41 a.m.

He'd better stock up on whisky. Ella's mother was the next blot on the horizon. A bombastic hard-drinking woman in her mid-sixties, she had recently divorced her long-suffering second husband and replaced him with a trainee barista a third her age. They were coming to lunch at the weekend and he was thinking of pasta; he was simply too busy and tired for anything else but Ella wouldn't be pleased.

It was hard, the way older women got better with age while men lost their sexual allure. It was an unfair fact of nature. Our skin is so much coarser, he reflected, prone to early furrows and open pores and sag; and then of course – unfairest of all – we go bald. Nobody really respects a man any more once he turns forty, particularly if he's losing it on top.

3:48 a.m.

And the media is so disparaging of men over forty, he thought; the way it zooms in on our paunches and spindle shanks, our pendulous earlobes. Another real worry was, he was developing turkey wattles. Ella had noticed it too – she'd called him jowly the other day, she'd pinched an incipient fold of flab while ostensibly chucking him under the chin.

Why can't there be some positive older role models for a change? he fretted. Wherever you went, images of young men in next to nothing were in your face, making you feel bad about your body. His route to work was tyrannized by giant posters of ripped abs, honed six-packs, buff biceps.

In a pathetic attempt to fight back, he'd recently been engaging in a spot of newsagent guerrilla warfare. Now when he bought his paper he made sure to stick some of his pre-prepared Post-it notes to the naked boys on the covers of the women's magazines – notes he had felt-tipped in advance with the words: WHAT IF HE WAS YOUR SON?

3:50 a.m.

Moving deeper into the forest of worries, his mind now fixed on Colin's silence and pallor. He'd shown signs of shaky self-esteem from early on, his boy Colin, and now, at the age of thirteen, it seemed he might be flirting with anorexia. There was the other thing too, which was even more worrying, the cutting thing, but he wasn't going to mention that to Ella yet.

Whereas Daisy, at nine, knew exactly what she wanted and it definitely didn't involve self-excoriation. She was obsessed, already, with the most brainless computer games, all about domination and detonation. She needed ferrying round for miles at weekends for her competitive yoga, which she was taking to county level – there was talk of trials in Birmingham, Ella was very thrilled. Not that he resented this for a moment; he was proud of her too, of course he was, and he was able to get on with his marking while he waited outside various sports venues for the necessary hours. But it would have been nice to get a thank-you once in a while.

He really must stop bleating.

What a loser! No wonder Colin's self-esteem was low with *him* as a role model.

Was he managing to be a good father to him? That was what really worried him – him and the other dads. They all agonized endlessly about whether or not they were good fathers.

4:04 a.m.

His heart was very slow, wasn't it? It felt like it was labouring up a hill. Thump. Thump. Thump.

Now it was racing! Something must be wrong. He wasn't over-joyed about still being on the Pill.

All four of his grandparents had died of strokes or heart attacks, but Ella couldn't tolerate condoms. They muffled things, she said.

4:08 a.m.

While he was getting undressed last night she'd had the cheek to say, 'Those pants are getting tired.'

'They're not the only ones!' he'd flashed back, the worm turning, keenly aware that it wasn't just his pants that were being criticized.

Afterwards she had rolled off him and fallen asleep with a snore.

4:13 a.m.

He knew he really should think about his own satisfaction as well but somehow it was so much easier at the time to concentrate on gauging her levels of interest and to adapt himself to what worked for her. The trouble was, he himself needed some patience and encouragement – he found it really didn't work for him without at least five minutes' foreplay.

'Oh for God's sake, get it up and get on with it,' she'd snapped at him the other night – though, to give her her due, she had apologized soon afterwards. Still, he couldn't help resenting her impersonal demands for sex; her obdurate refusal to talk, ever. Then there were her smothered belches, the semi-stifled farts she seemed to find so hilarious, not to mention the mulch of underwear she left in her wake or the state she left the bathroom in on a nightly basis. It was like the stables at the end of the world once she'd finished with it.

4:21 a.m.

A bird had started up outside, and light was looming round the edges of the curtains. He closed his eyes without much hope and began to count apples on an imaginary tree.

4:22 a.m.

No, that was no good. Try the one which made him tired just to think about, the one where he was climbing the steps of a spiral staircase which he saw was endless.

He knew Ella watched porn online. That was why she was so late coming to bed – 'Just checking my emails.' She didn't know he knew and he wasn't going to tell her, but there was the evidence on her laptop when he tapped into it – Loaded Lunchbox, Bollocks 'n' Bunfights, all those fit and perfect men.

He understood the arguments: it's completely mainstream; everybody looks at porn; it's just another way of relaxing. But something in him protested against it.

'Don't be such a MasculiNazi,' Ella said if he ever said anything. He hated it when she called him that. But it's important that we get more men out of prostitution, he'd been saying; that we get more men into Parliament. 'Of course it is, darling,' she'd replied indulgently.

To be fair, she did sometimes listen to him rant on about the injustice of the system. She even agreed with what he said, which was after all based on facts, incontrovertible. But she had no interest in changing it. Why would she when it worked so well for her?

4:30 a.m.

He could see how he had to come last in the family pecking order. Something had to give and it wasn't going to be Ella. And he couldn't bear it to be the children.

He minded that she rode over him roughshod, that she made all the big decisions, the ones about money and hours, without consulting him. The last thing he wanted was to be accused of being shrill, though, and anything he said to contradict her did not go down well at all.

4:33 a.m.

It all made him feel rather depressed. Which accounted for the chocolate he squirrelled away round the house. A good woman is hard to find, he was in the habit of reminding himself as he broke off another row of Fruit & Nut. This didn't help shrink his paunch one bit, but he had to have something.

4:42 a.m.

'Is it just that women aren't as nice as men?' he'd blurted out at the last Book Club meeting.

'They're certainly more ruthless than us,' Mike had said, looking pensively at his fingernails. 'The real difference seems to be that they're able to compartmentalize. They can cut off. And of course they're more ambitious.'

'I'd be ambitious too if it was allowed!' Dave had laughed.

They had all laughed at that.

'It's the famous old triple conundrum,' Dave had continued. 'You can have two out of three but not three. You can have the woman and the job, or the woman and the children. But you can't have the woman *and* the job *and* the children.'

'Why not?' he'd persisted. '*Women* don't have to choose! Why can they have it all and not us?'

'That's life,' Dave had shrugged.

5:11 a.m.

It was about power, really, in the end – but he'd never thought of himself as a political person. Ella wouldn't talk about it. She wouldn't put herself out to talk to him, or to listen to him either. 'Childcare?' she'd yawn if he asked her for a couple of hours off. 'That's your job.

Just do it!' She'd say it in an ironical way – obviously! – but even so he'd find it difficult to laugh. She was big on irony; she frequently got irony to do her dirty work for her. Then she'd accuse him of being humourless.

He could feel rage bubbling up in spite of himself.

'You're so *angry*,' she'd chided last time he'd complained. 'It's very unattractive.'

5:20 a.m.

He was holding the lime-green digits in view, and gave a little moan as they flicked on to 5:21 a.m. He had been stretched over this mental gridiron for what felt like hours, tossing and turning until he was scorched on all sides. No chance of sleep now. Ella was snoring away beside him on her unassailable barge of slumber. Rage swept through him. YES he was angry! Here he was, lying in bed worrying, scrolling back through the week wondering what steps he could take to improve things between them; and here she was, impervious, complacent, sleeping like Queen Log.

Surely she should make an effort too? If she loved him? Didn't she see how unfair it all was? Surely she'd noticed how his vitality had had to be progressively tamped down, year on year, since the arrival of their first child? This unilateral decision to preserve her life in its pristine state within their marriage – untrammelled by domestic duties or family admin – when had it been taken? How had he been persuaded into colluding?

Well, it was either that or leave. *She* wasn't going to give an inch.

He loved her, he wanted her respect. He knew she loved him too, really; what puzzled him was how she could be happy to exploit him in such a blatantly unequal set-up.

'I know you'll do things if I nag for long enough,' he'd said to her on their last holiday. 'What I really want, though, is for you to take on some of the worrying. Some of the actual work, the thinking and feeling.'

'But I know you'll do that for me,' she'd smiled back. And she'd been right.

So it was generally agreed that men were nicer than women, less selfish, more caring; men had been awarded the moral high ground. Big deal! And was that supposed to make everything all right? He twisted in the dark, the acid reflux of injustice rising in him. The world wasn't going to change just because he wanted it to, though, was it. The world was woman-shaped – get over it!

7:10 a.m.

When he woke up, everything was exactly the same as it had been the night before. Of course it was; unimaginable that it wouldn't have been. And there would be absolutely no point in dragging any of these night thoughts up into the daylight, he decided as he drew the curtains; nothing was going to change. This was the way things were. This was the natural order. ■

PHOTOGRAPH BY MARY ELLEN MARK, *ACROBATS REHEARSING THEIR ACT AT GREAT GOLDEN CIRCUS,* AHMEDABAD, 1989

Develop your creativity, tell your stories, and gain skills essential for personal and professional development in the **FICTION WRITING DEPARTMENT** AT COLUMBIA COLLEGE CHICAGO.

FICTION WRITING & PLAYWRITING DEGREE PROGRAMS

- **BA in Fiction Writing**
- **BFA in Fiction Writing**

- **BA in Playwriting**
- **BFA in Playwriting**

- **MFA in Creative Writing – Fiction**
- **MA in the Teaching of Writing**
- **Combined MFA/MA**

Our renowned Story Workshop® approach emphasizes voice, imagery, audience, and positive reinforcement of your strengths as a writer. Check out **colum.edu/fiction**, or call **312 369 7611** for info on our diverse study programs, extensive course listings, award-winning student anthology *Hair Trigger*, and visiting writers series.

create...

Columbia
COLⱢEGE CHICAGO

YOUR STORIES.
YOUR FUTURE.

Columbia College Chicago admits students without regard to age, race, color, creed, sex, religion, handicap, disability, sexual orientation, and national or ethnic origin.

THE SEX LIVES
OF AFRICAN GIRLS

Taiye Selasi

B egin, inevitably, with Uncle.

There you are, eleven, alone in the study in the dark in a cool pool of moonlight at the window. The party is in full swing on the back lawn outside. Half of Accra must be out there. In production. Some fifty-odd tables dressed in white linen table skirts, the walls at the periphery all covered in lights, the swimming pool glittering with tea lights in bowls bobbing lightly on the surface of the water, glowing green. The smells of things – night-damp earth, open grill, frangipani trees, citronella – seep in through the window, slightly cracked. You tap the glass lightly and wave your hand, testing, but no one looks up. They can't see for the dark. It rained around four for five minutes and not longer; now the sky is rich black for its cleansing. Beneath it a *soukous* band shows off the latest from Congo, the lead singer wailing in French and Lingala.

She ought to be ridiculous: little leopard-print shorts, platform heels, hot-pink half-top, two half-arms of bangles. Instead, wet with sweat and moon, trembling, ascendant, all movement and muscle, she is fearsome. It is a heart-wrenching voice, cutting straight through the din of the chatter, forced laughter, clinked glasses, the crickets. She is shaking her shoulders, hips, braided extensions. She has the most genuine intentions of any woman out there.

And they.

Their bright *bubas* adorn the large garden like odd brilliant bulbs that bloom only at night. From the dark of the study you watch with the interest of a scientist observing a species. A small one. Rich African women, like Japanese geisha in wax-batik *geles*, their skin bleached too light. They are strange to you, strange to the landscape, the dark, with the same polished skill-set of rich women worldwide: how to smile with full lips while the eyes remain empty; how to hate with indifference; how to love without heat. You wonder if they find themselves beautiful, or powerful? Or perplexing, as they seem to you, watching from here?

The young ones sit mutely, sipping foam off their Maltas, waiting to be asked to dance by the men in full suits, shoving cake into their mouths when they're sure no one's looking (it rained around four; no one sees for the dark). The bolder ones preening, little Aunties-in-training, being paraded around the garden, introduced to parents' friends. 'This is Abena, our eldest, just went up to Oxford.' 'This is Maame, the lawyer. She trained in the States.' Then the push from the mother, the tentative handshake. 'It's a pleasure to meet you, sir. How *is* your son?' You wonder if they enjoy it. You can't tell by watching. They all wear the same one impenetrable expression: eyebrows up, lips pushed out, nostrils slightly flared in poor imitation of the 1990s supermodel. It is a difficult expression to pull off successfully, the long-suffering look of women bored with being looked at. The girls in the garden look more startled than self-satisfied, as if their features are shocked to be forming this face.

But their dresses.

What dresses. They belong on the cake trays: as bright, sweet and frothy as frosted desserts, the lacy 'up-and-downs' with sequins, tiny mirrors and bell sleeves, the rage in Accra this Christmas. It's the related complications – tying the *gele*, the headwrap; wrapping then trying to walk in the ankle-length skirt; the troubling fact that you haven't got hips yet to showcase – that puts you off them.

You can barely manage movement in the big one-piece *buba* you borrowed from Comfort, your cousin, under duress. The off-the-shoulder neckline keeps slipping to your elbow, exposing your (troublingly) flat chest. Absent breasts, the hem drags and gets caught underfoot, a malfunction exacerbated by your footwear, also Comfort's: gold leather stilettos two sizes too small with a thick crust of sequins and straps of no use. You've been tripping and falling around the garden all evening, with night-damp earth sucking at the heels of the shoes, the excess folds of the *buba* sort of draped around your body, making you look like a black Statue of Liberty. Except: the Statue of Liberty wears those comfortable sandals and doesn't get sent to go fetch this and that – which is how you've now found yourself alone in the study, having stumbled across the garden, being noticed as you went: little pretty thing, solitary, making haste for the house with the shuffle-shuffle steps of skinny girls in women's shoes; and why you tripped as you entered, snagging the hem with your heel, the cloth yanked from your chest as you fell to the rug.

And lay. The dry quiet a sharp sudden contrast to the wet of the heat and the racket outside. And as sharply and as suddenly, the consciousness of *nakedness*. Eve, after apple.

Your bare breastless chest.

How strange to feel naked in a room not your own, and not stepping from the bath into the humidity's embrace, but here *cold* and half naked in the leather-scented darkness, remembering the morning, the rain around four. This was moments ago (nakedness) as you lay, having fallen, the conditioned air chilly and silky against your chest. Against your nipples. Two points you'd never noticed before but considered very deeply now: nipples. And yours. The outermost boundaries of a body, the endpoints, where the land of warm skin meets the sea of cold air. Shore. You lay on your back in the dark on the floor, like that, newly aware of your nipples.

Presently, the heart-wrenching voice floating up from the garden, '*Je t'aime, mon amour. Je t'attends.*' You sat up. You listened for a moment, as if to a message, then kicked off the sandals and stood to your feet. You went to the window and looked at the singer, in flight on the stage, to the high note. '*Je t'attends!*'

Indeed.

So it is that you're here at the window when, five minutes later, he enters the room, his reflection appearing dimly on the window before you, not closing the door in the silvery dark. You think of the houseboys with their lawn chairs in an oval reading *Othello* in thick accents, Uncle watching with pride. *Demand me nothing: what you know, you know. From this time forth I never will speak word.* (Likely not. With the thing come together, the pattern emerging, the lines, circles, secrets, lies, hurts, back to this, here, the study, where else, given the fabric, the pattern, the stars. What to say?)

Enter Uncle.

II

From the start.

The day began typically: with the bulbul in the garden, with the sound of Auntie shouting about this or about that, with your little blue bedroom catching fire with sunlight and you waking up from the dream. In it, your mother is bidding you farewell at the airport. This first part is exactly what happened that day. You are eight years old, skinny, in the blue gingham dress with a red satin bow in your braids and brown shoes. Uncle is in the terminal presumably buying your tickets. You are waiting with your mother on the sidewalk outside. She is crouching beside you with her hand on your shoulder, a wild throng of people jostling around and against you. Her fingernails are painted a hot crimson red. You are noticing this.

Blood on your shoulder.

Meanwhile, a stranger with a camera is trying to take a picture. She doesn't know your first name so keeps calling out, 'Child!' You've never once thought of yourself as this – 'child' – neither *a* child nor someone's; you've always simply been *you*. A smallish human being by the side of a larger one, both with neat braids with small beads at the ends; both slim (well, one skinny) with dark knobbly kneecaps; one never without lipstick, the other never allowed. In the dream, as it happened, you ignore the photographer. 'Child!' she calls louder. A dark, smoker's voice. Finally you look up in the hope of some silence.

'Smile!' She, unsmiling.

You consider, but frown.

Your mother pulls you close to her, so close you can taste her, the scent of her lotion delicious, a lie. It's a sensory betrayal the taste of this lotion, the smell on your taste buds not roses at all. A chalky taste, heavy and soapy as wax. You suck it in greedily. Swallowing it.

Her braids are tied back with an indigo scarf, the tail of which billows up, covering her face. The scarf is tied tightly, pulling her skin towards her temples, making her cheekbones jut out like a carved Oyo mask. The red on her lips contrasts the indigo perfectly, as the man who bought the scarf would have no doubt foreseen. Not for the first time you think that your mother is the most beautiful woman in Lagos . . . well . . . quite likely in the world, but you've never left Lagos and it hasn't begun to dawn on you that you will. That Uncle is in the terminal buying only two tickets, that she's not coming with you, that she hasn't said why. You don't think to ask. At this moment, here beside you, your mother is unquestionable. You simply don't ask. In the dream, as it happened, she kisses you quickly, her lips to your ear, and says, 'Do as you're told.' The stranger presses a button and the flash goes off – POP! – and your mother turns – POOF! – into air.

In the liminal space between dreaming and waking (into which enters shouting, about this or about that) you started to scream but the feel of the sound taking form in your throat woke you fully.

You wet the bed.

Now the terror passed over, with the cold in your fingers, the echo of POP! and your heart pounding, hard. To almost precisely the same beat someone leaned on a horn – HONK, HONK, HONK – at the front gates outside. You fumbled for the photo you keep under your pillow as an antidote of sorts to the dream (or the waking): the sepia shot of your mother and you, with her crouched so you're both the same height, cheek to cheek. The wildness of Lagos is an odd, knee-high backdrop: passing cars, people's legs, soldiers' boots, cripples, trash. But when you look at it now you see only your mother. The scarf blowing forward and hiding her face. She is sending you to live with your uncle 'for a while'. No one has heard from her since.

Still.

You wouldn't say your mother 'abandoned' you exactly; it was Uncle's idea that you come. It was the least he could do, the elder brother, her only sibling, after all that she'd been through, abandoned, pregnant and the rest. You've heard the Sad Story in pieces and whispers, from visitors from the village, whence the rumours began: that your mother got married and is living in Abuja with no thanks to Uncle and no thought of you. Not for a minute do you believe what they say. They are villagers, cruel like your grandmother.

As told to you:

Dzifa (missing mother) was born eight years after Uncle in Lolito, a village on the Volta. Their father, a fisherman, was drowned in the river the day after Dzifa was born. Their mother, your grandmother, for obvious reasons decided her daughter was cursed. Uncle, unconvinced, worshipped and adored his little sister and the two were inseparable growing up. Dzifa was beautiful, preternaturally so, shining star of the little Lolito schoolhouse. But your grandmother, believer in boys-only education and a product of the same, withdrew her daughter from school. Your mother, infuriated, ran away from Lolito and hitchhiked her way to Nigeria. In the same years Uncle won the scholarship to study in Detroit and left Ghana, himself, for a time. Dzifa found her way to, and met your father in, Lagos (a privilege – meeting your father – that you've never had). An alto saxophonist in an Afro-funk band, he left when he learned she was pregnant.

Enter you.

The brother/sister reunion came some seven years later when business brought Uncle to Lagos. You were living at the time in a thirteenth-floor hotel room, free of charge, care of the hotel proprietor. His name was Sinclair. At least that's what they called him. This may have been his surname; you were never really sure. He was ginger-haired, Scottish, born in Glasgow, raised in Jos, son of tin miners-cum-missionaries, tall and loud, freckled, fat. On the nights that he visited, at midnight or later, he'd hand you a mango, smiling stiffly. 'Go and play.'

It was always a mango, with perfect gold skin, which he'd pass palm to palm before tossing to you. He was stingy with his mangoes, barking at the kitchen staff in the morning to use more orange slices and pineapple cubes in the breakfast buffet. His face blazed an unnatural pink when he shouted, like the colour of his hair, or his skin after visits. (You were shocked when you moved here to find mangoes more perfect growing freely on the tree in the garden.) You'd go to the pool, glowing green in the darkness. The sounds of the highway, of Lagos at night. There were no guests or hotel staff at the pool after midnight. No sweating waiters in suits with mixed drinks on silver trays. No thin women in swimsuits, their skin seared to crimson, their offspring peeing greenly in the water. Only you. Still now there is something about those nights that you miss; maybe the promise of your mother in the morning? Hard to say.

On the night Uncle found her she was circling the lounge like the liquor fairy, topping up vodka and Scotch. You were behind the bar reading *Beezus and Ramona*, recently abandoned by some American. *Ex libris: Michelle.* It was a Friday, you remember: Fela blasting, men shouting, the lounge packed, Sinclair smiling, counting cash, your mother's laugh. Then abruptly, glass smashing, a comparative silence, the extraction of human voice from the ongoing din. The resumption of talking. You looked. There was Uncle. She was staring at him, mouth agape, shards at her feet. '*You*,' he was saying softly, then hugging her tightly. Over and over and over. 'Dzifa. *You*.' You'd never seen him before that night. You wondered how he knew her name. Sinclair wondered too and rushed over now, shouting, 'DON'T TOUCH HER!' while you watched, considering Uncle.

Your mother said nothing. After a moment she smiled. Too bright to be real. Too beautiful to be fake. After the hugging and weeping and telling it all Uncle insisted she return to Ghana. She refused. A compromise. Uncle would take 'the child' to Accra and when your mother was ready she would join you. You packed. Uncle and a woman, a fair-skinned Nigerian, the photographer, drove you to the airport. You'd never been. The woman smoked cigarettes. You'd seen her at the hotel once, her hands and neck darker than her bleaching-creamed face. Your mother was silent, gazing away, out the window, her eyes black and final as freshly poured tar. You were pressed up against her, so close you could breathe her, the taste of rose lotion breaking the promise of its smell.

Then Murtala Muhammed: the arriving, the departing, the begging, the crippled, the trash and the throng. Smile! Pop! Poof! Here you are three years later. End of Sad Story.

The morning.

You set down the photo and glanced out the window. The caterers had arrived with the party decor. A large painted banner on the back of their truck read *Mary Christmas!* in red and green letters. You laughed. Only then did you realize that you'd peed in the bed, as happens when the dream is most vivid. The warmth of the wet spot turned cold on the backs of your thighs.

Auntie screamed, 'You illiterates!'

'Please, oh, I beg,' one of the caterers placated.

'It's m-e-r-r-y. *Merry* Christmas.'

'Yes, Madame. Mary,' the caterer assured.

'No! That says "Mary". The mother of Jesus.'

'Jesus *is* Christmas.' As if he'd heard it somewhere.

Auntie sucked her teeth. 'May He help me.' The voices carried up from the gates into your room as you wiped off the backs of your legs with a towel. You detached the fitted sheet from the narrow twin bed and carried it, embarrassed, to the washroom.

III

Ruby was there sucking her teeth at the washer. She prefers to clean clothing the old way, by hand. Auntie will hear nothing of primary-coloured plastic buckets ('You're not in backwater bloody Lolito still, are you?'). Uncle bought the washer on his last trip to London, along with the blue jeans you've cut into shorts. He'd meant them for Comfort but they didn't quite fit as she's put on weight studying at Oxford. Auntie, who refuses to travel to Britain, waited for the delivery as for a prodigal child. (Auntie calls London 'too grey' for her taste. Comfort says Auntie feels 'too black' abroad. Whatever the case, none of your neighbours have machines as impressive as the one in the washroom. Ruby would say there's a reason for that but, like you, Ruby does as she's told. It was triumph enough when the washer's noisy brother, the dryer, was sold off for parts. The whirring contraption put too great a strain on the power supply, waning in Ghana.)

Ruby was dressed in the same thing as always: a T-shirt extolling the world to 'Drink Coke!' with a thin printed *lappa* and black *chalewatas*, the flip-flops Auntie buys in bulk for staff. No one seems to mind much that you wear them also. Comfort would 'nevah deign' to. (Nevah, without the 'r'.)

'Good morning, Ruby.'

Ruby said nothing. Frowning with her eyebrows but not with her eyes. She stands like this often, with her hands on her hips, bony elbows pushed back like a fledgling set of wings. She is pretty to you, Ruby, though her appearance is jarring, the eyes of a griot in the face of a girl. It's an odd mix of features: pointy chin, jutting cheekbones, tiny nose, initiation scars, village emblems. It's hard to tell what age she is. Her eyes have the look of a century of seeing. They say she lost a child once. (Which would certainly explain it. In the peculiar hierarchy of African households the only rung lower than motherless child is childless mother.)

'Fine,' she said finally. She held out her hand. You gave her the sheet, which she shoved into the washer. She closed the windowed door and looked, scowling, at the buttons, unsure which to press, too proud to say so. You came up beside her, pressed 'Gentle Cycle'. Silence. The washer, as advertised, sprang noiselessly to life. Ruby gasped, startled, stepping backwards. 'Eh-hehn!' You stepped back, too, to be next to her.

And stood. Shoulder to shoulder, like a couple viewing a painting. Whites in the window of the washer, sheets and shirts. The cloth twisting beautifully like the arms and long legs of the National Theatre dancers dancing silently in soap. Ruby sucked her teeth, repeated 'Fine', and left the washroom. She returned a moment later with a clean fitted sheet. You took this, folded neatly and smelling of Fa soap.

You said, 'Thank you.'

Ruby said, 'Hmph.' (But her eyes said, 'You're welcome,' and, briefly, she smiled. She is beautiful when she smiles. It isn't often.)

IV

From the washroom to the kitchen at the side of the house, the sun slanting in through the windows.

The door was propped open to the buzzing of flies and the symphony of the sounds of the houseboys in the morning: Kofi hanging the washing Ruby brings out to dry, blasting Joy FM on his transistor radio; Francis's little paring knife dancing on the chopping board, a staccato cross-beat to the bass lines outside; Iago, né Yaw, soaping the Benz in the driveway with the sloshing of cloth in the bucket of suds; and George, grumpy gatekeeper, at the end of his duties, eating *puff-puff* he buys at the side of the road. Your breakfast was laid on the small wooden table: one scallop-sliced pawpaw and lime wedge as always. Francis was frying *kelewele* for Comfort (her favourite) in honour of her first morning home. She's been in Boston for an exchange programme at Harvard since August. After Christmas she'll go up to Oxford again.

'Good morning, Francis.'

'*Oui. C'est ça,*' his standard answer, smiling, Francis, gentle giant, six foot six, a most unlikely cook. He'd been working in Accra's finest restaurant, Chez Guy, when Uncle discovered his *pissaladière*. To the dismay of his employer, the eponymous Guy, Uncle made Francis a better offer. His parents are Ewe, his mother from Togo, his English much weaker than his French, even now. 'Did you sleep good?'

'How *could* one?' Comfort. Appearing at the door in her slippers.

She padded into the kitchen, stretching her arms with a yawn. 'With Mother bloody yelling – is that *kelewele* I smell?'

'*Oui. C'est ça.*'

'Oh, how *good* of you, Francis.' With the exaggerated British accent. Frawn-sis.

'*Je t'en pris.*'

She plopped herself down at the table across from you. Reached for a slice of your pawpaw and sighed. 'And you, little lady.'

'Good morning.'

'Good morning. As skinny as ever. She only eats fruit.' Comfort picked up the lime wedge and sucked on it, rueful. 'Is Daddy awake?'

Francis frowned. '*Oui. C'est ça.*'

Auntie and Uncle take their breakfast on the veranda or in the dining room with linen and china and silver. Comfort and you have always eaten in the kitchen, the small one, at the rickety wood table like this. The arrangement dates back to the morning you arrived after the short Virgin flight from Nigeria. As he tells it, Uncle ushered you proudly into the dining room for breakfast. You don't remember any of these details. You wouldn't look up from your plate, as Francis tells it; you just sat there, mute, mango on fork tines. After Uncle tried unsuccessfully to sell you on an omelette Francis intervened, uncharacteristically. He lifted you carefully out of the dining-room chair and carried you into his kitchen. Like that. Silent, he placed you at the small wooden table and returned to his work pounding yam. For the next week you refused to eat any meal at all unless seated in 'Francis's kitchen', so-called. Auntie had a massive new kitchen installed off the first-floor pantry this summer. No one but Auntie much likes the new kitchen, though it's nicer, says Francis, than Guy's. Francis still insists upon preparing for meals – shelling beans, gutting fish – in 'his' kitchen.

'*Bon.* We couldn't well let you *starve*,' Auntie tells it. 'However pedestrian to eat with the help.' Comfort assumed she was missing something special, characteristically, and demanded to join you. When Auntie said no, Comfort refused to eat also, so Uncle said yes, but only breakfast.

v

Iago appeared presently at the door to the kitchen. He is the best-looking houseboy, you think. There's been talk of a liaison between Iago and Ruby but you don't believe a word they say. First, Ruby never smiles and Iago never stops: perfect teeth, strong and white, and one dimple. Second, she lost a child. Third, you're in love. (And what would they know about love in this house?) In addition to the beauty, and there is no other word for it – he's *beautiful* in the way that a woman is, insistent – he is clever. The cleverest of all, according to Uncle, who just last Monday said as much during Reading Group.

Uncle started the Shakespeare Reading Group last winter, with the dust like fine sugar on the grass, in the air. Auntie thinks it's ridiculous – 'Houseboys reading Shakespeare? I mean, *really* . . .' – but defers to him on this as on everything. Uncle's secretary Akosua makes the photocopies in his office then brings them to the house wrapped in paper. Kofi drags the lawn chairs into an oval by the pool, carrying out an armchair from the living room for Uncle.

They started with *Othello*. You found a copy in the study from Comfort's final year at Ghana International School. You read it in one sitting, seated cross-legged by the bookshelf. Uncle appeared so silently you didn't hear him. At some point you stopped reading and there he was. Uncle: arms folded, leaning lightly against the door frame. You uncrossed your legs quickly, fumbling to get to your feet, trying to think up an excuse for being in there. No one's forbidden you to enter the study – as you're forbidden, for example, to enter Auntie and Uncle's room – but no one's exactly invited you, either. It's your favourite room in the house.

On the one occasion Auntie caught you reading she said nothing. She was passing by your door on her way down the stairs. You were upright in bed by the window for light, reading Comfort's *House of Mirth*. She had a bottle of Scotch. She started to speak, hiding the bottle, then stopped. You pretended not to notice the bottle. She was staring at the tie-dye that's taped to your wall, as if suddenly transfixed by the pattern. You considered her. It was a new way of seeing her, your own gaze unnoticed, staring straight at her face while she gazed past, through yours. She looked young without make-up and tired. Even soft. The cream-satin nightdress, sponge rollers.

'That's Ruby's *lappa*, isn't it.' A statement, not a question.

'She gave me the cloth, for decoration,' you said.

'That was kind of her,' Auntie said. 'Ruby . . .' Then stopped. You waited for her to finish. She didn't. She stared at the tie-dye cloth (Ruby's old *lappa*, a worn piece of wax batik, blue with white stars, sort of misshapen stars, more like starfish), saying nothing, then abruptly looked away, as if remembering you were there. She said, 'You'll strain your eyes, reading in the dark like that.'

You didn't mention that you don't have a lamp. 'Yes, Madame.'

But she didn't forbid you to enter the study. You did and found the battered *Othello*. You were there sitting cross-legged when Uncle appeared at the door and you half tried to stand.

'Don't get up.'

His voice was so gentle, just barely a whisper, as if speaking too loudly might cause you to rise. 'Please, don't get up.' He laughed softly. He sighed. 'You look just like your mother.' He told you to keep Comfort's copy of *Othello*. He invited you to Shakespeare Reading Group that week. You went to the garden, read the part of Desdemona. The pool brilliant blue in the late-morning light.

George read Brabantio. Francis read Roderigo. Iago read Iago. But his name then was Yaw.

The best-looking houseboy, indeed.

It's the skin that seems edible, that insists upon being looked at, less the colour than the consistency, the constancy, and the eyes. You've only ever seen such eyes on Ashanti men with slender builds. Those narrow, twinkling, inky eyes, as thin and angled as Asians'.

Yaw made his announcement at the end of the hour with his hand on his packet as if the play were a Bible. 'From this day forth my name will be Iago.' Uncle asked why. 'He is strongest,' Yaw said.

Kofi raised his hand. 'Yes, sir?' Uncle said.

Kofi looked at Yaw, almost pityingly. Sighed. 'The *king* is strongest.'

'Impeccable logic. But Yaw is correct.' That one dimple. 'Iago you wish to be, Iago you are.'

Iago, né Yaw, in the doorway.

'Good morning,' he said brightly, leaning into the kitchen. He held out the mangoes to Francis.

'Good morning,' you said softly, turning from the table to face him, losing your breath for a moment at the sight. Comfort said nothing, her mouth full of *kelewele*, blowing out air – 'hot, hot, hot' – as she chewed. As a rule she isn't rude to the house staff (like Auntie) but she doesn't 'associate' either. Even to Ruby, who was employed before Comfort was born, Comfort says little. The only employee you've ever heard her thank that one time is Francis. She barely seemed to notice Iago, back-lit, at the door.

'You are welcome, Sister Comfort,' he whispered. She looked. The sun from behind him seeped into her eyes. Seated across from her, you stared at her face.

You'd never seen this particular look in her eyes, which are dark brown and gentle, even flat sometimes, still. Not empty, as such – not like Ruby's – but still, like the eyes of a cow, deep and sated. She looked up, saw Iago, and her eyes sort of flickered. Just the hint of a hardening.

'Morring, Yaw.' Her mouth full.

As you stare at her now through the wide picture window, looking down at the garden and your cousin in her lace, you think to yourself, as you thought at the table this morning, *it's a very pretty face*. Sort of heart-shaped and plumpish with the cheeks of a cherub, the long curly lashes and small, pointy chin. Her lips look like pillows, some unique form of respite: top lip and bottom lip equal, together forming an 'O'. She has Uncle's flawless skin, the same sparkle and shade as the earth after rainfall, as shea-buttered soft. The skin on her collarbones and shoulders, in particular, is impossibly smooth, with a specific effect: that calm kind of loveliness unique to flat landscapes, to uninterrupted stretches of uniform terrain. Perhaps in the absence of the absolute standard that is Auntie, you'd call Comfort 'beautiful'.

But there she is – Auntie – fluttering from table to round table, drawing all eyes and oxygen towards her, restless Monarch. She is somewhat less witch-like when viewed through the window. Merely beautiful beyond all reason. The long jet-black hair against skin that won't tan, wide-set eyes and the warpaint of cheekbone. For a moment you wonder if it's the beauty that's aggressive, perhaps in spite of its owner, and not Auntie herself? Perhaps anyone so striking, so sharp on the outside, would appear to be hard on the inside as well?

Then Auntie stands straight and the moon gilds her up-and-down: white in a garden of colour, as foreseen. As you watch from the study Auntie flutters to Comfort, who is fussing with Kwabena, her fiancé. Auntie offers her cheeks, one then the other, to his kisses. Comfort steps back, for no reason; there is space. Kwabena begins gesturing, chatting animatedly with Auntie. Comfort sips foam off her Malta, gazes away.

She isn't lovely near Auntie; you see this now, plainly. She couldn't be lovely. She is too starkly lit. It isn't that Auntie casts others in shadow, as you've often heard it said. It is the opposite. She is luminous. A floodlight on everything around it, in darkness. In an instant something lights Comfort's eyes.

It is the same thing you saw for that moment this morning, the sun slanting in thick and golden as oil. That flash, like two fireflies in Comfort's black pupils, while Iago wiped his hands on his trousers, looked down.

Francis finished crafting a blossom from an orange then turned his focus to scalloping mango. He gave the overripe mangoes to Iago as he does despite Auntie's weekly speech on 'free lunch'. You finished your pawpaw, surreptitiously watching Iago, his *chale-watas* wet still from washing the car. The pink tip of his tongue on the stringy-gold flesh, the wetness around his mouth, made your stomach drop down. A feeling very similar to wetting the bed when the dream is most vivid. The dampness and all.

Iago finished the mango and tossed the pit across the kitchen. It landed in the rubbish with a clatter. '*Gooooooooooooooooal!*' Francis called out like a football announcer. You giggled. Comfort slapped at a mosquito.

'Is Madame in the garden?' Iago asked, licking his fingers.

You nodded. 'With the caterers.'

'Bloody party,' Comfort said. She considered the mosquito

bite blooming on her arm. 'Damn mosquitoes. Every Christmas. For what?'

'I go and come.' Iago, backing away from the door. He ran down the path along the side of the kitchen.

This scraggly grass walkway runs between the house and the Boys' Quarters, the staff's modest barracks, half hidden in brush. On the other side of the house is a wide pebbled walkway that winds from the gates to the garden at the back. This is how party guests access the garden. The house staff, forbidden, use the kitchen path. It scares you for some reason. Its dark smell of dampness, the wild, winding crawlers climbing the side of the house, the low-hanging tree branches twisted together like the skinny gnarled arms of a child with lupus. And, set back in shadow behind the tangle of branches, ominous and concrete, never touched by the sun: those three huddled structures with their one concrete courtyard where the houseboys sit on beer crates and eat after dark. If you're passing the round window on the second-floor landing you can look down and make out their shadows at night. A cooking fire flickering against the black of the sky and their laughter in bursts, muted refrains. No one's ever forbidden you to join them, to go back there. But no one's ever invited you either. They scare you: the Boys' Quarters, the trail through the thicket.

Iago disappeared down this path.

You took your plate to the sink, turned on the water to rinse it. Francis patted your head, took the plate, pushed you away. Your willingness to do housework is an oddity at Uncle's, as the notion of house staff is an oddity to you. *You* who ate leftovers at the bar with the busboys at the end of each night while your mother drank rum; who helped maids on the mornings your mother was hung-over; eating left-behind chocolates and half-rotting fruit. But Ruby doesn't need or want help with the washing. Iago will let you trail him reciting *Othello* across the lawn (he has memorized his part and no longer needs a script), as Kofi will abide your quiet audience. Francis will let you watch from the little wooden table while he skins and chops chicken in the afternoon light. But no one will allow you to *do* what you're watching. It was Kofi who one day read from his script: 'Blow, blow, thou winter wind! Thou art not so unkind as man's ingratitude.' You'd been trying to hang your sheet on his line outside the kitchen. A breeze had kept billowing it up. Francis finished breakfast and arranged it on a tray. As if on cue, Ruby came into the kitchen, *chale-watas* slapping the concrete. She stopped when she saw Comfort. A small curtsy. She didn't smile. 'Miss Comfort. You are very welcome home.'

'Morning, Ruby.'

Ruby, to Francis: 'Madame already took breakfast?'

He handed her the tray. 'Only tea.'

'Will she eat?'

'She's fasting for the party.' Comfort sucked her teeth dramatically. 'That's my mother. *Bon.*' It was the briefest of glances: Ruby's eyes lifting sharply, darting quickly to Comfort, then snapping back down. Comfort didn't notice. Ruby left with Uncle's breakfast. The swinging door flapped lightly back and forth, then shut behind her.

Comfort turned to Francis, scratching the mosquito bite on her arm. 'Kwabena is coming for pre-party cocktails. I told him I'd make him that *chin-chin* he likes.'

'*Mais bien sûr, mademoiselle.*' Francis began wiping the counter.

'Bloody bugger. Still thinks I can cook.' Comfort laughed. 'I haven't seen him since August. I was slimmer then, wasn't I?' She sucked at the bite as it started to bleed. She looked at you jealously. 'Not like you. But still slimmer.'

You shook your head, lying, 'You're still the same size.'

She beamed as if with delight at your very existence. Then, suddenly remembering: 'I brought some books back from Boston.'

'You did?'

'Yes, of course. They're in the study. Go and get them.'

'Don't do that, please.' Iago. Appearing at the door. He leaned in (the houseboys don't enter the house) and held out an aloe leaf to Comfort, cracked open. She looked up and frowned. The little flicker again. Confusion? Irritation? But smiled politely.

She went to the door, took the leaf from his hand. 'Aloe,' she said, sounding confused.

'For your arm,' said Iago, backing away from the door. Suddenly shy. Disappearing. Comfort watched him go, rubbing her arm with the sap. 'Has Iago gotten taller?'

'*Oui. C'est ça.*'

VI

The study is at the end of the second-floor hallway at the opposite end from your bedroom. Its one wall-length window overlooks the back garden, the three other walls lined with books. Uncle's large desk and stuffed chair face the vista, the chair with its back to the door. And the rug. Every room in the house boasts a thick Persian rug, courtesy of Auntie's (estranged) Uncle Mahmood. In the study – as in the parlour, as in the dining room, as in the drawing room – this furnishing serves to mute footfalls.

The door was half closed when you came for the books. Comfort said, 'Go and get them,' and you did as you were told. The swinging door clapped shut as you bounded out of the kitchen. Up the staircase to the study, skipping every other stair. You were wondering what books Comfort had brought back from Boston, whether more Edith Wharton or your new favourite Richard Wright? The door was ajar but no sunlight spilled out of it. You approached and peered in the slim opening.

The drapes were pulled over the window, uncharacteristically. Uncle's breakfast tray, balanced at the edge of the desk. The plates were all empty, Francis's blossom destroyed. A stack of glossy paperbacks beckoned by the tray.

You assumed, perfectly logically, that Uncle had finished eating and left the tray for Kofi or Ruby to come collect. You pushed the door slightly and slipped in the slim opening, your feet sinking into the soft of the rug.

Uncle was in his chair, facing the window and drapes, gripping the edge of the desk with his fingertips. From your vantage behind him across the room in the doorway you could barely see Ruby between his knees. She was kneeling there neatly, skinny legs folded beneath her, her hands on his knees, heart-shaped face in his lap. The sound she made reminded you of cloth sloshing in buckets, as rhythmic and functional, almost mindless, and wet. Uncle whimpered bizarrely, like the dogs before beatings. For whatever reason, you stood there transfixed by the books.

It was Ruby who saw you but Uncle who cried out, as if sustaining some cruel, unseen wound. Now you saw the trousers in a puddle around his ankles. Now he saw you, mute, at the door. He grabbed Ruby's head and pulled it away from his lap. She crumpled to the rug like a doll.

'Stupid girl!' he spat. 'Get out! Get out!' Whether to you or to her, you weren't sure.

Ruby scrambled to her feet; you stumbled back out the door. She wore only her *lappa* and a tattered lace bra. She looked at you quickly as you pushed the door shut. Her almond eyes glittered with hatred.

You recognized the expression. You'd seen it once before, in the morning in Lagos with your mother and Sinclair. You'd been loitering in the kitchen waiting for the cooks to finish breakfast. Just as Francis does with Iago, they'd slip you anything spoiled: collapsed soufflé, browning fruit, crispy bacon, burned toast. The trick had been to show up after Sinclair made his rounds, shouting complaints then disappearing until dinner. The spoils that morning had been unusually abundant: enough fruit for a week, pancakes, over-boiled eggs. A younger cook had set the food on a metal rolling cart and sent you up to your room in the freight elevator.

The rest you remember not as a series of events but as a single expression. A postcard. You must have inserted the keycard in the door, which would have beeped open, blinking green, making noise. But they must not have heard you. So you wheeled in the cart and just stood there, frozen, mute at the door.

That expression.

Your mother on the floor, Sinclair kneeling behind her, their moaning an inelegant music, the sweat. Her eyes open wide as she looked up and saw you, surprise that you'd returned from the kitchen so soon. And the hatred. Bright knives in the dark of her irises. Unmistakable. You'd left the cart, running.

From the study to your room.

Slamming the door, leaning against it. The sound – sloshing cloth, buckets of soap – in your ears. Your bright blue walls trembled, or seemed to, in that moment, like a suspended tsunami about to crash in. The image (not yet a memory) – of Uncle in his desk chair; of Ruby folded prayerfully on her knees between his – flashed on the backs of your eyelids like a movie whose meaning you didn't quite understand. But you saw. In that moment, as you stood there, with your back to the door and the lump in your throat and your pulse in your ears, you saw that it was *you* who was wrong and not they. You were wrong to have pitied her. Ruby. That she could make Uncle start whimpering like the dogs before beatings meant something was possible under this roof, in this house; something different from – and you wondered, was it better than? preferable to? – the thing you lived out every day. You envied Ruby something, though you didn't know what. You stood at your door trembling jealously.

Someone approached.

You heard the steps (small ones) on the other side of your door, followed by the faint sound of feet on the stairs, going down. You waited for a second then cracked the door open. No one was there. You looked down. Someone had stacked Comfort's paperback books on the threshold. Like a fetish offering. You glanced down the hall to the study; the door was open. The drapes had been drawn back to richly bright light. You picked up the books and you walked down the stairs. The meaning – whether Uncle's or Ruby's – was clear.

So you went to the garden as you would have done otherwise, had you not seen what you saw in the study just then. You said nothing to Francis who was just starting the *chin-chin*, nor to Iago who was making centrepieces of torch gingers as you appeared. You didn't so much as gasp when you found Comfort by the pool on her back on a towel in a bikini.

You stopped, staring down at her. She shifted, squinting up at you.

'I see you got the books,' she said.

You nodded. Quietly: 'Thank you.'

'You're welcome.' She smiled. Then closed her eyes. Without opening them: 'You're in my sun.'

Caterers swarmed the garden, unfolding round wooden tables, festooning lights along the walls, ignoring Comfort by the pool. The garden half done like a woman getting ready, standing naked at the mirror in her necklace and shoes. The thick buzz of flies and the sweet smell of *chin-chin*. Not for the first time you thought about running. They were consumed with their preparations, all of the houseboys and caterers, Comfort sunning in her bikini, Iago working by the pool. You could get up now, unnoticed, leave your books, walk away. There was the door at the edge of the garden.

You'd always wondered where it led to; it was always closed and no one used it. You considered it, suddenly hopeful, not one hundred yards away. Perhaps it pushed out to some Neverland? To Nigeria? Or simply to some route to the road through the brush? You were considering the distance from the tree to the door when the thought seized you suddenly: but what if she's gone? What if they were right, and she'd run off to Abuja, with no thanks to Uncle and no thought of you? Now the breath left your chest and your heart began racing. To almost precisely the same beat, someone's hammer: THWAP! THWAP! Two carpenters installing the dance floor, banging nails: THWAP! THWAP! while your chest refused air.

And there was Auntie.

She was standing across the garden at the door into the living room in big bug-eye sunglasses, shouting your name. The way she scanned the garden made it clear she couldn't see you where you crouched behind the veil of tree leaves, silent, trying to breathe. She was starting to go in when she saw Comfort by the pool. 'For God's sake, daughter. What are you doing?'

Comfort lifted her head, shading her eyes with her hand, the flesh at her mid-section folding over. 'I'm sunbathing, Mother. It's good for my skin.'

'You're going to get darker.'

'Yes, likely.'

'Don't be smart. Your husband is coming this afternoon. You need to get dressed.'

'My *fiancé*.' Comfort lay back down, adjusting her position on the towel. Auntie glanced at the caterers, who were observing this exchange. 'What are you looking at?' Nobody answered. Auntie snapped, 'Where *is* that girl?'

An inhalation at last. 'I'm here, Madame,' you called hoarsely, stumbling out from the leaves. She glanced at you casually, as if you'd always been standing there. Then looked down at Comfort, sucked her teeth, turned away. 'Kwabena is coming. You had better be decent.' Over her shoulder, to you, 'Ehn, let's go.'

VII

Makola Market is thirty minutes' drive from the house. You sat in the back, silent, with Auntie. You glanced at her quickly, holding her bag in your lap, trying to interpret her vacant expression. Did she know that this morning after serving Uncle's breakfast, Ruby removed her little shirt and knelt between his knees? Would Uncle send you away if you shared this with Auntie? Would Auntie like you better if you did?

You were thinking this over when she spoke. 'When I call you, you come. Do you hear me?'

'Yes, Madame.'

The market was crowded with Christmas returnees haggling unsuccessfully over the prices of trinkets. And the fray. The bodies pushed together in the soft rocking motions; the sellers shouting prices over heaps of yellowing fruit; the freshly caught fish laid in stacks of silvery carcasses, their eyes still open wide, as if with surprise at being dead. You pushed through the traffic to the back of the market and parked outside Mahmood the Jeweller's.

Mahmood is Auntie's uncle, one of the richest men in Accra and the nicest you've met apart from Francis. He used to call you 'Habibti', as if it were actually your name, and bring you *ma'amoul* wrapped in wax when he visited. His houseboy Osekere would lug in a case of Chateau Ksara and they'd sit by the pool, drinking: Auntie, Uncle, Mahmood. Two or three bottles down, Mahmood would demand that you join them, instructing Kofi to come get you from your bedroom. Never Comfort.

He liked to tell the tale of the silkworm crisis that brought the Lebanese to Ghana. You'd lean against his stomach while he stroked your hair, talking. English Leather, fermented tobacco, citronella in your nose. The last time he visited – over a year ago, summer – you climbed into his lap as per habit. He stroked your knee gently and kissed you on the head. 'Habibti.' He wiped powdered sugar from the *ma'amoul* off your lip. 'Have I ever told you the story of Khadijeh the silkworm?'

'No,' you lied, giggling.

'Have I not?' Mahmood laughed. Uncle pulled on his cigar, his eyes twinkling in the candlelight. 'Fucking silkworms.'

'Watch your language,' Auntie hissed.

Uncle merely laughed, ignoring Auntie, speaking louder. 'Might have been silkworms that sent you damn Arabs but it was British worms who welcomed you, them and our women.' He removed his cigar slowly and smiled, not kindly. 'You've made whores of them. All of them –'

'Not in front of the child.' Auntie glanced at you.

Laughing harder. 'She's my sister's daughter,' Uncle said. 'She of all people understands what a whore is.'

Then silence.

Their eyes grazed your face and you closed your own tightly but no sooner had you done so than the image appeared. On the backs of your eyelids where such images are stored: of Sinclair on the floor with your mother. You opened your eyes quickly but the image remained.

You were sick to your stomach. There were hands at your waist.

'Don't mind them, Habibti,' Mahmood whispered softly. He was squeezing your waist tightly then kissing your cheek. His beard scratched your shoulder. His lips wet your neck. The thought was just forming: his hands are too tight. They were pressing against your ribs through your nightdress; you were nauseous. You'd eaten too many pastries – and that word in your mouth. That image in the air. *Whore*. You started to speak. But heard Auntie as you opened your mouth.

'DON'T TOUCH HER!' she raged at him, leaping to her feet.

'Sit down, Khadijeh!' Uncle, leaping to his. The gesture knocked his glass to the tile where it smashed. The wine ran into the pool like a ribbon of blood. 'You will *not* address a guest in my house in that manner.'

Kofi jumped back. Auntie gasped. Mahmood chuckled.

'*Malesh*, Khadijeh. *Malesh*,' he said calmly. He stood, lifting you with him, kissed your head, set you down. 'Go inside, Habibti,' he whispered, ruffling your hair. 'Go inside. Sweet dreams. I'll see you soon.'

But you haven't.

He hasn't been to the house since that night by the pool and neither Auntie nor Uncle so much as mentions him.

You trailed behind Auntie to the door to the store. A sign read: 'Back after lunch. *Shukran*.' She pushed the door lightly. It opened. A bell jingled. You entered. No one materialized. 'Hallo?' she called out.

You lingered behind Auntie, glancing at your reflections in the mirrors. She in her sunglasses. You, shorter, in your shorts. In light like that there is something very African about Auntie. Her skin is so pale you often forget that she's half. But the set of her mouth, the slight downturn of the lips, the proud upturn of the chin betray her paternity.

Her eyes met yours suddenly. You looked away quickly. 'What are you looking at?'

'I wasn't expecting you,' someone said. Both you and Auntie turned to the back of the store where Mariam, Auntie's mother, stood watching her. In spite of yourself you took a little step backwards. She is terrifying to you, Mariam, viscerally so. She has the same dramatic features as her daughter and brother, her skin a dark bronze from the decades in Ghana. It's the dark hooded eyes that deny her face beauty: the slope of the eyelids, the black bushy brows. They say that Mahmood would be nothing without his sister, ruthless bookkeeper; that it was she who built his business. Mariam said nothing. She just stood at the counter at the back of the store watching Auntie. She didn't so much as look at you.

'I can't see why you wouldn't "expect" me. We throw the same party every year.' Auntie sighed. 'Aren't you at least going to offer us tea?'

You stiffened. You didn't like the sound of this 'us'. But Mariam smiled brightly, a menacing expression. A bit like a wound beneath her nose. Her eyes travelled past Auntie and rested on you. Without irony: 'May I offer you tea?'

To watch Auntie now on the dance floor with Kwabena, her see-through lace glowing like sun-tinted ice, it doesn't seem possible, what you heard next from Mariam. It is obvious, and still seems the lie. This has less to do with Comfort – who sits sipping her Malta, watching Auntie dancing with Kwabena as the singer wails in French; and whose eyes, more like Ruby's than you'd previously appreciated, are up-lit by candles and sparkling with spite – and more to do with Auntie, who is laughing now, clapping, while the other dancers, sheep, start to laugh and clap too.

This is what jars you as you watch from the window: how impervious she appears still, impenetrable. There is anger in Auntie and, you see it now, hurting. The sheen of her eyes like a lacquer, sealing grief. But the appearance is compelling, the apparition of Auntie's fortitude. Bright black-haired chimera. It wants to be believed. And you want to believe it. The lie of her majesty. That she couldn't be other than what she appears. The truth of her weakness leaves nothing to be hoped for, leaves nothing to cling to, makes everything as weak. Meaning that something is possible here in this house where you envy the housegirl but don't know for what – and it's not what you thought, which was that you were forsaken, alone. It is that all of you are.

Mariam, to you: 'May I offer you tea?' How you ended up overhearing from the bathroom. You followed her up that dark, narrow back staircase to the office above the shop, which you'd never before seen. It was filthy: a cluttered office with a kitchen in the back, sticky tiles, one oily window overlooking the market. Mariam went to the kitchen and put a kettle on the stove. Auntie stood looking around as if for a mop. Finally, she perched gingerly on the arm of a desk chair. She gestured to you, impatiently. 'Bring the invitation,' she said.

You opened the handbag and pulled out the envelope. Mariam reappeared with two teacups. 'Tea,' she said. She handed you both cups, took the invitation, looked it over. Then sat at the desk clasping her hands. You handed Auntie a teacup. There was no place to sit. You wished you had waited with Kofi in the car. You didn't dare ask now. No one moved. No one spoke.

'Keeping up appearances,' Mariam said finally. 'Well done.' She has Auntie's clipped accent. She didn't have tea. You noticed this now, peering into your own teacup with worry. Mariam noticed your expression and chuckled. 'Poison-free.'

'Oh, for God's sake. Let's not start.' Auntie hissed. 'I'd like you to come to our party tonight. People ask questions when you don't.'

'Let them ask. You've embarrassed your family. That's all there is to it.'

'That's not what you said when I married him.'

Mariam sneered, 'This isn't about Kodjo.' She said the name with contempt. 'If you lie down with bush boys you get up with fleas.'

'Well, you would know –'

'How *dare* you? Your father was different! An honourable Ghanaian. A *very* good man.' Mariam pounded the desk with her fist on this 'very', her face flushing mauve and her eyes welling up. The outburst made you start, spilling tea on your T-shirt. They both turned to look at you now.

'Please excuse me,' you mumbled. You stood, glancing at Auntie. She said nothing. Mariam said, 'Go,' and you went. Through the kitchen into the bathroom where you closed the door quickly, then instantly wished that you hadn't. There were flies in the toilet and stains on the tiles, the stench overwhelming: urine, ammonia, mothballs. You were fumbling with the door, trying to let yourself out, when Mariam began screaming on the other side of it. 'You disrespect my brother in that philanderer's home –'

And Auntie: 'You can't be serious. Your little stand-off is about Mahmood?'

'*Uncle* Mahmood, kindly. After all that he's done.'

'Which is what, Mother? Kindly. Do tell.' Auntie laughed.

'You know bloody well that he paid for your schooling.'

'For my schooling. For my *schooling*?!' Now Auntie's laughter was shrill. 'Is that the going rate for a virgin in Ain Mreisseh?'

'Go to hell.'

'Thank you, Mother.'

'You're a liar.'

'I was twelve.'

'It's your husband who insults you, running around with those bush girls.'

'At least they're grown women.'

Mariam laughed, genuinely amused. 'The daughter of a housegirl. Passed off as your child. And is she? A comfort?'

'You know why I can't.'

Auntie said it very simply, in a very small voice that you'd never heard her use but could match to an image: of her standing in your doorway in pale pink sponge rollers, transfixed by the *lappa*, unbearably frail. Her words and their meaning were like a taste on your tongue, then, a thickness spreading slowly across the roof of your mouth. *The daughter of a housegirl. You know why I can't.* You heaved, vomited pawpaw into the toilet.

Silence.

Now came a rustling, someone slamming a door; now the clicking of heels, growing louder, towards the bathroom. From outside the door: 'What the hell are you doing?' You wiped off your T-shirt, cracked opened the door.

There was Auntie, crying quietly, fumbling for her sunglasses in her bag. She looked at you blankly and turned. 'Ehn, let's go.'

VIII

You got in the car. She got in the car. Kofi glanced back at her, started the car. She removed her bug sunglasses and wiped her eyes quickly. She put them back on. She said nothing.

Kofi pulled up to the gates and honked. George opened the gates with much clanging of locks. Kofi drove in, Benz tyres crunching white pebbles. Auntie said, 'Thank you,' got out. You'd never heard her thank anyone for anything before. Kofi said, shocked, 'Yes, Madame.'

You're still not sure why you followed her in. She got out on her side and you jumped out on yours. Perhaps you were waiting for instructions about something? About not saying a word to a soul or suchlike? Watching her now on the dance floor with Kwabena, it occurs to you that you didn't want to leave her alone. You needed to stay near her, you thought, trailing behind her.

So you followed her into the kitchen.

Francis was removing a tray of *chin-chin* from the oven. You entered behind Auntie, swinging door swinging shut.

'I told you to cook in the new kitchen,' she said. Francis looked up, startled.

'Madame?'

'I told you to cook in the new kitchen,' Auntie repeated. 'Not in here. In this dump. With these flies. Do you hear?' Francis shook his head in confusion. Auntie stepped forward to stand just beneath him. 'No, you don't hear me? Or no, you don't understand me? Or no, you intend to ignore me? You, too?' She was laughing hysterically. He shook his head, faltering. Then Auntie reached up and slapped him. Once.

He dropped the tray of *chin-chin*, the sweets scattering across the floor. Tears sprung to your eyes.

And to his. And to hers. She stabbed the air in front of him, gasping for breath. 'You do as I tell you. You do as I say.'

Then walked out of the kitchen, started sobbing. You stood there with Francis, who stared at you, silent. With tears in his eyes and what else? Was it anger? You'd never seen him angry. You tried but couldn't speak. For the thickness in your mouth. All the words. The door opened suddenly and Uncle stormed in. He looked at the *chin-chin*, scattered nuggets on the floor. 'Idiot.' To Francis. 'Clean up,' as he left.

The sky seemed to darken outside the door.

Francis knelt down and picked up the tray – a long way down for such a tall man. He set it on the counter, leaving the *chin-chin* on the floor. He ducked, and walked out the door.

You waited too long. There, dumbstruck in the kitchen. You waited too long before you followed him out. You dropped Auntie's bag and ran out the side door but you didn't find Francis so you ran down the path. You hurried through the thicket along the side of the kitchen between the house and the Boys' Quarters to the garden, crying now. The rocks and knotted roots cut through the soles of your *chale-watas* as you pushed through the low-hanging leaves. The sky was dark.

The caterers were raising a new banner above the dance floor. *Marry Christmas!* A boy was setting tea lights into bowls. No one seemed to notice you. You didn't see Francis. You saw the little door across the garden.

The door opens easily. Not to Neverland, it turns out, but to the unkempt brush of the neighbours' back lawn. Weeds, chopped-down trees, redolent dankness of earth. And Iago kissing Comfort in her bikini. She was leaning against a tree with her hands at his waist. He was cupping her breasts. He was shirtless. At the sound of the door creaking, feet crackling on twigs, Iago turned. He said, 'No.' Nothing else. Comfort looked also, saw you, and cried out. Iago clamped his hand over her mouth.

For the second time that day you backed out of a door, pulled it shut, and stood staring, now seeing. Four o'clock. There were your books, beneath the mango, where you'd left them. Thunder, then it started to rain.

You came up the path slowly in the driving rain, the wet on your shoulders and face like a weight. The smell of damp earth swelling up from the ground as it does in the tropics, overpowering the air. So that all that there was for those few wretched minutes was the rain on your skin and the earth in your nose. The caterers, behind you, shouting about things getting wet, as you pushed through the low-hanging branches, then stopped.

There, through the brush, in the Boys' Quarters courtyard beneath the one shower: there was Francis, soaking wet. With the water from the shower and the downpouring rain and the soap on his face, and the cloth in his hands. And his form. You gasped to see it, that foreign landscape of muscle: the hills of the stomach, the mountain of bum, the plain of his shoulders, the tree trunk of torso, the roots of the cordons the length of his legs. In a way, it was too much to see in that moment, through the tangle of branches, nude Francis. You turned.

But the sound of the movement was loud and he heard it. He turned his head quickly and opened his eyes. He stared at you, frozen, the cloth in his hands, but not using it to cover himself, suds in his eyes. '*Regardez!*' he called out through the brush and the rain. '*Je suis un homme, n'est-ce pas?*'

Now it stopped raining, as suddenly as it had started. As if God turned a tap just once to the left. Francis stood staring at you, arms open wide. The shower still running. With rage in his eyes. You could barely see anything, for the tears welled in yours. You turned and ran into the house.

Through the kitchen.

Through the side door into the kitchen, with the oven standing open, the spilled *chin-chin* on the tiles and Auntie's bag on the floor. To the stairs, past the washroom, where the caterers were conferring noisily about the soaking-wet linens, decrying the absence of a dryer.

Up the stairs to your bedroom, where you removed your wet T-shirt, kicked off the sopping *chale-watas*, pulled on your cut-offs, a dry top. You found the slippers with the beading, beckoning cheerfully, slipped these on. You squeezed your eyes shut. But couldn't breathe. So opened your door.

Auntie was on the stairs, her eyes swollen, no make-up. She glanced towards your bedroom. You retreated too late. 'Whatever are you wearing? There's a party tonight.'

'I'm changing,' you said softly.

'Into what?'

'A Christmas top.'

'And the trousers?'

'I can press them.'

'You'll do nothing of the sort. Borrow a *buba* from your cousin.'

'Yes, Madame.'

'Your hair is wet.' She continued down the stairs then paused abruptly, looking up. 'And where *is* your cousin?'

'I'm right here,' Comfort said.

She'd appeared at the base of the stairs in her robe, wearing Iago's *chale-watas*, many sizes too big. Auntie looked at Comfort then back up at you. Comfort looked up at you also. (And you couldn't for the life of you see how you'd missed it. Comfort looks nothing like Auntie.) Their eyes on your face, different shapes, the same pleading. Auntie turned to Comfort and pointed at her shoes. The *chale-watas* looked bizarre on Comfort's delicate feet.

'And whose are those?'

'Mine,' you answered quickly.

Auntie sighed. She considered your cheerful slippers, considered Comfort, and hissed. She continued down to Comfort and lifted her chin. 'We'll never bloody marry you off at this rate.' She dropped Comfort's chin and walked off.

Comfort looked up, at you. 'Do you not speak English? Get dressed, Mother said. There's a party tonight.' But she didn't sound angry and just stood there, started crying. 'Thank you,' she mouthed to you.

'You're welcome,' you said. She is beautiful when she smiles. It isn't often.

IX

Enter Uncle.

He walks in behind you, saying nothing at all and not closing the door in the silvery dark. You turn round to face him. Full circle. Explaining, 'I was fetching an album for Auntie. I'm sorry.' Your *buba* slides down. You start to say more but he holds up a hand, shakes his head, is not angry.

'It's nice to be away from it all. Isn't it?' He smiles.

'Yes, Uncle.'

'I'll bring her the album. Relax.' He joins you at the window. Ever so slightly behind you. Puts a hand on your shoulder, palm surprisingly cold. In a very gentle motion he rearranges the *buba*. 'Are you happy?' The question surprises you.

'Yes, Uncle.'

'What I mean is, are you happy here? Happy living here?'

'Yes, Uncle.'

'And you would tell me if you weren't?'

'Yes, Uncle.'

'Meaning no.'

'No, Uncle.'

'"No, Uncle." Better than "yes", I suppose.' He chuckles almost sadly. He is quiet for a moment. 'Do you miss her?'

'Yes, Uncle.'

He nods. 'Yes, of course.' Then you stare out the window, another couple at a painting. The singer is hitting a high note, clutching the mike as if for life. You look at the dance floor. You see Kwabena but not Auntie. The younger girls dancing with men in full suits. You look to the tables. There is Comfort, sitting stiffly. Iago, in a server's tux, approaches with drinks. He pours her more Malta; Comfort doesn't look up. You feel your breath quicken. Uncle's hand on your neck.

'You remind me so much of your mother.' He leans down now. The hotness of rum and his breath on your skin. The *buba* slides off and he adjusts it again carefully. 'She had this long neck. Just like yours,' he says, touching. You stiffen. Not at the touch but the tense. He notices. 'I frighten you,' he says, sad, surprised.

'No, Uncle.'

'Bloody hell. Is that all you say?' He speaks through clenched teeth. 'It's a *question* for God's sake. Do I frighten you?' You are silent, unable to move. '*Answer* me.' Not gently, he turns you round. Unable to face him you stare at your feet sinking into the carpet, toes painted pink. But when he lifts your chin, whispering, 'Look at me,' you do – and don't find the anger you're expecting. None at all. You have never been this close to Uncle's face. You have never noticed its resemblance to your mother's. The dark deep-set eyes. And in them something familiar. Something you recognize. Loneliness. Loss. 'I didn't frighten her,' he says insistently, slurring the words. 'I never frightened her. Do I frighten you?' Your chin in his hands.

You shake your head quickly. 'No, Uncle,' you mumble.

'I miss her so much.' He cups a palm around your cheek. And when he leans down to kiss you, you know what he means. You feel his tears on your face, mixed with yours, warm; his cool. There is something sort of disgusting about the feel of his lips, as there must have been something disgusting to Auntie about Mahmood's. But you bear it for those moments, as an act of generosity (or something like it), feeling for the first time at home in his house.

Still, you can imagine how it must look from the doorway when you hear Auntie, 'How long does it take –?' then sudden silence as she sees. 'Oh, God,' she splutters out in a horrified whisper. The only sound in the darkness. 'Oh, God.'

Uncle pulls away from you and looks at his wife. 'Khadijeh.' And there is Auntie, in the doorway. How she falls. She leans against the door frame then slumps to the ground. She repeats the words, 'Oh, God.'

Close to hyperventilating. In tears. Uncle smoothes his trousers with the palms of his hands. He touches your shoulder calmly before going to the door.

'Khadijeh,' he says, kneeling, but she pushes him away.

'Don't touch me. How dare you? God damn you to hell.' She hits him now, desperately. 'She's your *blood*. She's your *blood*.'

'That's enough,' he says softly, as she kicks at his shins. He grabs her by the shoulders, standing her up on her feet. She flails at him, sobbing. He slaps her. Hard. Once. 'This is *my* house,' he says. Walks away.

In the dark and the silence you wish you could vanish, at least crawl beneath the desk without her noticing and hide. But she barely seems conscious as she sits in the doorway, her lace like a pile of used tissues, a cloud.

And that's when it hits you. Your mother isn't coming. Wherever she's gone it's a place without *life*. What life there was in her was choked out by hatred; whatever light in her eyes was the glint of that hate. And whom did she hate so? Her brother? Her mother? Your father? It doesn't matter. They live. She is dead.

This is what you're left with: a life with these people. This place and these women. Comfort. Ruby. Khadijeh. Who – it suddenly occurs to you, with an odd kind of clarity, as you watch from the window – mustn't be left to die, too.

So you go to her, stumbling over the hem of the garment as you cross the Persian rug and she looks up, face smeared. The kohl make-up runs down her cheeks like black tears. You sit down beside her, laying your head in her lap.

'Edem,' she whispers faintly.

'Yes, Auntie.' You start to cry. A familiar sound, peculiar: the sound of your name. You put your arms around her waist. It is softer than you'd imagined it. You hold her very tightly, and she holds you as if for life. You wish there was something you could say, to comfort her. But what? In the peculiar hierarchy of African households the only rung lower than motherless child is childless mother. ∎

OTHER WOMEN

Francine Prose

This is the story I tell: In the spring of 1972, I was twenty-five years old, unhappily married and living in Cambridge, Massachusetts. Like many women I knew then, I joined a feminist consciousness-raising group, to which I belonged for six months until I left my husband and moved across the country. A year later, when I briefly returned to pick up some possessions, I learned that, after my departure, my husband had serially and systematically slept with all the women in my group.

He'd been my college boyfriend and was a graduate student in mathematics. We'd gotten married during my senior year. The day before the wedding, my mother said, You can still call it off. Though I would have liked to, it seemed like too much trouble. I knew the marriage was a mistake. The hot buzz of romance had worn off, and there we were, stuck with each other at a historical moment when – or so we heard – the so-called sexual revolution was boiling all around us.

Another mistake: after college, I went to graduate school, where I spiralled into a long, persistent, low-grade nervous breakdown. Officially, I was a PhD candidate in medieval English literature. Unofficially, I was a semi-agoraphobic stoner who stayed in bed for days watching TV and tried never to leave the house except to attend an intermediate Latin class I needed to fulfil a language requirement. The class was on Ovid's *Metamorphoses*, which I truly loved, but I failed all the quizzes and eventually stopped going.

Among my terrors was the fear of a certain street near my apartment. For some reason the block had become an impromptu gathering spot for flashers who sat in cars and exposed themselves to young women passing by. What scared me was not the sight of their pink, innocent-looking genitals but the looks on their faces, the paradoxical mix of shame and goofy ecstatic triumph.

Feminism was big news then; a groundswell political movement. Gloria Steinem was a star. Literary celebrities – Kate Millet, Germaine Greer – were created overnight, lost classics were resurrected. There were public and private conversations about the truly egregious ways in which women were underpaid, underrated, excluded from certain professions and restricted to others. Such things were debated on talk shows!

One thing people said was: The personal is political. It was an attractive idea because it suggested that the most quotidian events were reflective and emblematic of the dramas enacted in the wider world. Of course, this is true, and it isn't. Having a stranger assume you are stupid simply because you have a vagina is related to the problem but is *not the same problem* as being subjected to an involuntary clitoridectomy. Sometimes it wasn't clear to me how well this difference was understood, but the general feeling was that if you looked at (and got together and talked about) how women were treated as second-class citizens in the home and office and classroom, your perspective would broaden to include societies in which women were bought, sold, altered, bred and worked like barnyard animals.

Everywhere, women were staging protests, issuing manifestos, publishing newsletters that represented a broad spectrum from separatist radical lesbians to moderates who wanted respect, equal pay and a seat at the table. Like any social change, this one whipped up a mini-tornado of opposition: Norman Mailer had no problem writing that books by women (including Virginia Woolf) were humourless, sentimental, narrow-minded and unreadable. The more judicious worried about the damage to the American family if moms put their kids in day care and went out and got jobs. To be fair, there were excesses on both sides: women used words like *foremother* and *phallocratic* with straight faces and had debates about make-up.

I too began to question certain things I'd taken for granted. I noted, for example, the passive hostility of the distinguished professor who asked me, with disinterested curiosity, why women students were always in the dead middle of the class and never at the top or the bottom. Why couldn't I remember once seeing my father clear the table, even though he and my mother both worked long hours as doctors? Was my slide into marriage, graduate school and madness the result of an early indoctrination by *Cinderella* and *Jane Eyre*? Were the flashers on Kirkland Street only the psycho-expression of the outer reaches of men's true feelings about women?

And so it happened that I joined a consciousness-raising group. A possible explanation for my psychic decline had suggested itself: the too-early marriage, the too-easy path, the phobias and the weed. Had I wound up in this sorry state *because I was a woman?* This was the sort of question a women's group was supposed to address as we compared our experiences with those of our new-found sisters.

I don't know what I expected. A new way of being, I guess. Once we identified and divested ourselves of the bogus values imposed on us by the patriarchy, everyone would be equal and helpful and *nice to each other*. Our consciousnesses would be raised!

Half a dozen women, all in their twenties or early thirties, met in each other's homes (I always tried to persuade them to meet in my apartment) to talk about feminism in general and our lives in particular, to discuss the books and essays that had become iconic, and to report on our successes or failures in teaching our boyfriends or husbands how to use a vacuum cleaner.

Though I have hazy memories of some women in the group, I'm fairly sure that most were connected to the university or living with someone who was. Some were working or looking for the sort of young-people jobs (arts administrator, lab assistant) that suggest that adulthood will have some relation to one's college major. As I recall, only one of us had a child: a sweet woman with a nice husband; they both seemed overwhelmed. I remember two slightly older married women with stable lives and nicer apartments and a maternal but slightly judgemental air that made the rest of us want to please them. Then there was the pretty one, who'd brought me into the group.

The first disappointment was the rapidity with which we fell into roles that replicated junior high. As much as we critiqued the ways in which male culture had taught us to objectify our bodies, the same hierarchies applied: the plump deferred to the thin, the short to the tall, the homely to the handsome. The older women exerted a subtle maternal leadership, though the actual mother, the overburdened one, was considered slightly pitiful for having gotten herself into that situation. I also assumed a familiar role, a fallback position from grade school. Self-protective, watchful, stiff with social discomfort, at once too proud, too removed and too lazy to mention the phobias, the cannabis, the TV, the forlorn marriage, the secret novel forever 'in progress'.

None of that rose to the surface as I joined my sisters in complaining about the patriarchal creepiness of the men I knew. I described how my husband used to torment me by staring theatrically and somewhat apishly at every beautiful woman we passed until he was sure I noticed and then he would give me a horrible smile, like the rictus grin of the Kirkland Street flashers. I wondered why the other women so often rose to his defence and asked why I was being so hard on a guy who was tall, reasonably nice, intelligent and so forth.

If I'd imagined that the group would collectively generate a higher *consciousness* about ourselves in relation to other women and men, I soon realized we'd recreated in microcosm the Darwinian power relationships of the boardroom, the cabinet meeting, the office, the nursery school.

We too had our outcast: the future social worker's wife. Objectively, she was as smart and attractive as anyone else. But her mistake was being too honest and unguarded about her motivation for joining the group.

She made the mistake of saying what no one else would admit. She was sick of her marriage. Her perfectly pleasant husband had been her first lover. And to quote John Berryman, she was heavy bored. My guess is that all of us were bored and erotically restless; my sense is that the madly-in-love didn't rush to join women's groups.

But the obsessiveness and nakedness of this woman's discontent allowed the rest of us to pity her, to condescend and patronize her for focusing on something trivial and self-indulgent. When conversation lagged, the meetings devolved into scenarios in which she bemoaned her romantic ennui while the rest of us rolled our eyes and smirked. Watching her, I was reminded of the schoolyard lesson about the risks of volunteering too much information. But secrecy has its drawbacks, too – it can make you feel cornered.

Backed into a corner, I began to joke around – some of my jokes were funny, some not, some appropriate, some not. Some were probably hostile. No one else thought they were funny. I remember suggesting we read Valerie Solanas's *SCUM Manifesto*, a book I still think is hilariously weird. I especially loved Solanas's fantastic suggestion (I might be getting this slightly wrong) that the only way for men to rehabilitate themselves was to gather in groups and ritually chant in unison, 'I am a lowly abject turd!'

I remember telling this to the group. I recall no one laughing. A current joke was: How many feminists does it take to change a light bulb? Answer: That's not funny. But it wasn't the women's fault. None of them were stupid. Some had a sense of humour. They could tell that I wasn't trying to amuse but to provoke.

All this time, though sick with loathing and doubt, I was working on my novel. I wrote a first draft and put it away and rewrote it from scratch. Eventually, I got brave enough to show it to a former college professor.

Then, an unexpected event occurred. An editor called from New York. My former professor had sent him my novel, and he wanted to publish it.

A single phone call affected my brain like a jolt of ECT without the mouth guard, the electrodes or the memory loss. It was a miracle cure. I moved to San Francisco.

And so I returned a year later to collect my things. And that was when I found out that my husband had, so to speak, worked his way through the group. One of the women told me and excused herself; she wasn't the only one! No wonder he'd always seemed so pleased when the group met at our house. No wonder they'd always taken his side.

In fact, this was not how it happened. In fact, I'm pretty sure that my husband only slept with two of the women in the group.

I don't know why I tell this story, or tell it the way I do. Obviously, saying *all the women* in the group makes a better story than saying *two of the women in the group*. But under the circumstances, two seems like more than two, two seems like more than twice as much as one. It seems like a *statement,* which it was. I know he slept with the pretty one and (I think) one of the maternal know-it-alls and for good measure both of the girls who lived in the apartment upstairs in our weathered Cambridge three-decker.

If our true desires and disappointments are buried deep in our dreams, they're closer to the surface in the stories we tell and retell, in the mythologies we ourselves have come to believe. Does saying *all the women* express how betrayed I felt by my husband and my feminist sisters?

Actually, I was surprised by how little it upset me. Though I hadn't had the encyclopedic sexual experience that people of my generation are supposed to have had, I'd had enough to know: sex trumps politics, common sense and better judgement. And my husband's bad behaviour wasn't entirely unexpected. One gift of a faltering marriage is a heightened sensitivity to the frequencies of flirtation. And however misused, the word *liberation* was very much in the air, often to mean having sex with someone because it was more trouble to say no.

The truth is that when I think of that time, I feel neither outrage nor betrayal but gratitude: My consciousness was raised. Do I think that women are better than men and that the world would be a better place if women ran it? I can thank my Cambridge women's group (along with Margaret Thatcher and Indira Gandhi) for having cured me of the notion that women are no more or less likely than men to treat people well or badly. Perhaps the problem lies with institutions rather than people, and a group, no matter how small, is an institution.

Yet somehow, in the process, I became a feminist. Almost forty years later, feminism is as basic to my sense of self as the fact that I have brown eyes, as integral to my sense of the world as the fact that gravity keeps us from flying off the planet.

Do I think that women deserve equal pay for equal work? Do I think women are as smart and capable as men? Do I think that women are still being discriminated against in obvious and subtle ways? Does it disturb me to meet young women who imagine that the playing field is level and that feminism is irrelevant to their domestic lives and careers? Do I think women need to help one another? Have I noticed that there are men who inevitably and consciously or unconsciously treat women like idiots, babies or witches? Of course, the answer to these questions is an emphatic yes.

No matter how much or how little happened in those consciousness-raising groups, they were part of a formative era that opened the eyes and changed the minds of women like myself. Living through that time persuaded me not to think that gender discrimination is the unavoidable product of boys being boys. Along with consciousness came the faint consolation of knowing that certain slights and omissions, certain unenlightened attitudes and intended or unintended insults are neither purely personal nor in our imaginations.

I feel fortunate to have spent my adult life in the company of a (second) husband and two sons who actually like women – or, anyway, some women. But frequently when I venture beyond my domestic bubble, I'm reminded of the degree to which the weather is still chilly out there for the ladies.

Recently, I participated in a reading tribute to an important (dead white male) American writer. A friend sent me a link to an online literary site in which the presumably young male blogger noted (inaccurately, but whatever) that I was *taller* than any of my fellow readers, all male. Even as I was persuading myself that a similar comment might have been made about a five-foot nine-inch man (Gee, Philip Roth is tall!), I read further, to find myself described as acting like a 'socialite'. A *socialite*? *Me*? Don't socialites organize charity balls and nibble low-cal salad lunches and make cameo appearances on *Real Housewives of New York City*? Did he mean *sophisticate*? *Aristocrat*? Was he trying to be nice and got the wrong word? No matter how I parsed it, I couldn't imagine a male writer of my age with a similar publication record being described as a tall socialite. Or was it that the sight of a tall, reasonably competent woman inspired the blogger to think of Tom Wolfe's social X-rays and lemon tarts – women asking the waiter to bring the dressing on the side?

If I still belonged to my women's group, I could tell them that story and perhaps be heartened by stories of similar things that happened to them. Who knows where they are now? If their problems were solved or not, if they found jobs or not, had kids or not, left their boring boyfriends or not? All are older, some may be grandmothers and some may be long dead.

It makes for a better story to say that they all slept with my husband. But whatever symbolic or metaphoric truth the fictive version exhumes, I don't much care if it happened that way or not. I learned more than I would have if my feminist sisters had loyally resisted my former husband's advances. Gender doesn't confer moral superiority, nor the opposite, needless to say.

In retrospect, my women's group provided a political education, though not exactly the one that the women's movement intended. I learned not to follow a party line, I learned not to take things for granted or at face value, I learned to assume that situations may not be what they appear – all useful lessons for a novelist and a human being.

I don't know how much the group helped confirm my inconvenient determination to keep talking about the unpleasant or abysmal ways in which girls and women are treated. That inequalities and horrors continue to plague women is a fact, not my opinion. Though it is also true that many women's lives are vast improvements over what they would have been in 1972.

I remember asking my husband why he slept with all those women, and I remember him saying that he'd wanted to, all along. He gave me that wicked little smile, like the men in the cars.

By *all those women*, we meant *two women*. For me to claim that he slept with them all is not only untrue but also unfair. But it's the sort of embellishment that shines light on some deeper truth, in this case the peculiar truth of a long-ago skirmish in the ongoing, counter-productive war of men against women. ∎

Inheritance

1945, Bijnor, a man went door to door with
a basket of leeches. He never shouted his arrival
like the ice-candy man calling *Ice!*
Instead, the basket came unannounced, he'd
set it down when the door opened, *Is there*
illness in the house? My father was five,
his mother had a fever, it was too early
to know she was dying.
While four sons crouched behind her, the lid
was raised, flat bodies scuttled. One was lifted,
the head a translucent valve, with what
my father thought were very tiny teeth
it bit her arm and fell when it was full.
It made the sound of
a small balloon dropping. My father
tells this story like all others, slowly.
I am to learn something from it.
It was before Partition. We were
poor. We had no camera. The basket is shut.
Your mother dies. You leave Bijnor.
You will have a daughter
who will never stand in a doorway
with her arm held out.
She has no courage.
But she takes the stories she is given.
She tells them the best she can.

HOT-AIR
BALLOONS

Edwidge Danticat

Sherlon, my former philosophy professor, calls and says, 'Clio, my dear, I need a big favour from you.'

I can tell by the way he drags out my name and slurs on the word 'dear', that his nostalgia for our long nights on the bright red velvet couch in his faculty apartment has been inflamed by a great deal of alcohol. What I can't tell is whether he's just missing me, drunk-dialling to flirt, or has gotten himself into serious trouble. Maybe he's taken too many sleeping pills while polishing off a bottle of Chardonnay, thinking that this will bring either me or his estranged daughter back.

'What do you need?' I ask, sounding off-putting on purpose, even while calculating how long it would take me to get out of bed, slip out of my pyjamas into real clothes, and drive the fifteen minutes to his place.

'It's Polly,' he says.

He had foolishly convinced his daughter to leave her mother and her life in New York to attend the small private college in West Palm Beach where he was the philosophy chair. He had done it, in part, to have his daughter close to him, but she'd interpreted it as a desire to save money and she had dropped out in the middle of the second semester of her second year to join a small women's organization called Kenbe, Hang On, which ran a rape crisis clinic in Port-au-Prince, Haiti. He had not heard from Polly for weeks and neither had I, even though we'd been good friends before she discovered, from a casual remark he made while cooking a dinner for the three of us, that he and I were sleeping together. Her disappearance had given me an excuse to stop seeing him, something which I could never quite find the courage to do, even after a year of saying to myself that what we were doing was wrong, because he was my professor, because he was twenty years older than I was and because his daughter was my room-mate. Polly's absence made us both feel dirty and any conversation about her took away our desire to touch one another. Still, every now and then he would call me in a drunken stupor, in the middle of the night, to complain about some unrelated problem, mostly his students and classes, and I would listen to him while talking myself out of going over to his place and just holding him and apologizing for pushing his daughter out of both our lives.

'What's going on with Polly?' I ask. The fact that he was saying her name at all meant that something had changed either in her status, or ours.

'Her mother's not heard from her,' he says. 'She's not been calling me, but at least she had been calling her mother.'

The mother had long changed status, where he was concerned, from being his ex-wife to simply 'Polly's mother'. The way he said the word 'mother', especially when he was sloppy drunk, made me feel that Polly's mother had reached the lowest point of gradual erasure. It was dangerous to fall from his good graces. He could easily eradicate you with words; wipe you out of his life by merely shifting a pronoun or placing emphasis on a verb.

'What do you need me to do?' I ask.

Part of me is hoping to hear him say, 'Get in the car and come to me. Don't bother changing out of your nightgown. I need you now and only you can save me.'

Except he would never put it that way. If it came to that, he might say more professorially, 'For everyone's highest good, please come over.' This would give him a chance to tap into the past lessons he'd tried to teach me both in and out of the classroom: to entertain thoughts that I didn't completely accept, to find truth not in certainty but in ambiguity.

'You know Polly's mother's heart is not very good,' he says. Unlike most people who liked to trash their exes, he preferred to point out her myriad health problems as though they were weaknesses in her character.

'You know she has that strange condition where her gall bladder shoots small stones into the rest of her body,' he used to tell me. 'You know one of those stones nearly shut down her kidneys.' 'You know she nearly inhaled one of those pebbles into her lungs.' 'You know one of them attacked her heart.' He said this as though she had left herself wide open to all of that, as though she'd simply decided to commit gradual suicide by initially neglecting all the stomach and backaches that signalled the beginning of her decline.

'You know Polly's mother can barely walk now,' he says. 'She's being looked after by a nurse, and insurance being the crap it is in this country, she's paying out of her own university pension for the care. She's sick and nearly destitute and supremely depressed already, the last thing she needs is more complications in what's left of her life.'

He had married Polly's mother when they were both graduate students at the City University of New York. Her specialty was Caribbean history, which, according to him, she'd decided to study as a way of better understanding their Trinidadian background. They married in their early twenties, he told me, reasoning that it would be easier to live on very little if they merged into one household. Polly came early in the marriage, a surprise that would cause research papers to be late and classes to be missed and dissertations to be delayed by several years. He and his wife didn't agree on many things. Unfortunately, he realized this after the marriage, and even more so after Polly was born. The only thing they could agree on was their approach to parenting, which was loose and relaxed and resulted mostly from their being too busy with their academic work. Polly became as uninterested in them as they had appeared to be in her, throwing herself into her schoolwork with a zeal that they, scholars both, should have admired. Instead, as she had herself told me, they kept encouraging her to explore what they vaguely termed her 'artistic side', offering no guidance or direction, or even a suggestion.

Ambivalent parenting, she had called it, in her merely above a whisper of a voice. 'Should I have just woken up one morning and written a novel? I was never sure what they wanted from me. I had a feeling that if I stayed out of their way, they'd consider me a good daughter.' Still, when her father suggested after the divorce that she attend the small liberal arts school where he was teaching, she had been eager to give it a try.

'At last, he told me what to do,' Polly had said.

'There are plenty of children who come out fine *because* their parents didn't bully them,' he said. 'This is just who she is.'

His judgement was particularly cloudy for someone who considered himself a philosopher, but ask anyone about the tip of their noses – if they try too hard to study that island of skin, the rest of the world becomes blurry.

'Don't you think Polly is now complicating her mother's life?' he asked me.

'Do you really want me to answer that?' I said.

He relished in the rhetorical even when it didn't make sense. I felt like diving into an argument about it just to annoy him. Of course I didn't think Polly was complicating her mother's life. She was complicating her own life more than anyone else's. But he knew both Polly and her mother better than I did and maybe he was right about all of this in a way that I would never understand.

'What do you want me to do?' I settled deeper into my bed, while searching in the dark for the outline of the identical oak bed that had been his daughter's. It was still as well made, with hospital corners and fluffed pillows, as she had left it the night she'd walked away. Her books were still neatly lined up on the small bookshelf on top of her ink-stained desk. Crowding her bookshelves were novels for her Latin American literature class. She had bought an entire semester's worth of books using one of her father's credit cards. He had only come to our room to pick up her laptop, which was open to a half-written page on what she was calling the Death of Magic Realism. Could magic ever be real? she had noted, or reality ever be magical? She seemed to have been brainstorming and had gotten stuck. Maybe it was the magic realism paper that had driven her out of our lives. Maybe her father and I had nothing to do with it. That thought was only comforting for a moment. The rest of the time I would imagine her locked up in a room somewhere, hostage to some evil do-gooder who'd lured her with promises of saving poor Haitian women, only to keep her handcuffed to a bed. During more lucid moments, I'd imagine her leaning over a pew in a stone-walled open-air cathedral, wearing a nun's habit. I still couldn't understand though, what he wanted me to do. The long silences between sentences were not helpful either. Was I supposed to guess what was in his heart? What was in hers?

'Clio, I lied to Polly's mother and I told her that Polly had called me,' he said in his most professorial voice. He had that rare gift of sobering up quickly, or seeming to, like someone who had emptied a cup only so he could fill it up again.

'Should you have done that?' I asked rhetorically.

'Are you asking me something?' he said.

This was the way we always spoke. He could have the most violent reaction, slamming the phone down on me, if I told him straight out what he should or should not do. Now that we were broken up, I could say whatever I wanted. His punitive silences were not supposed to affect me.

'I don't think you should have lied to your ex-wife,' I said.

'There's a grave real possibility that something terrible might have happened to my daughter,' he said. His voice cracked and for a second it sounded as though he was crying. Then he broke into a loud laugh and I realized that he was doing both, laughing and crying at the same time.

I have replayed over and over in my mind the night Polly left his apartment. He was nearly done with the salad and pholourie balls that would accompany his stewed chicken and rice, when she asked in the type of timid voice that one might use to address a stranger, whether he was going to be leaving town during his sabbatical the following year or whether he would be one of those professors who stick around and come to the department a few times a week and end up working anyway.

'Maybe I'll do something wild,' he replied. 'Join an ashram or get a butterfly tattoo on my ass cheek like Clio here.'

I could tell that he wished the words hadn't come out of his mouth as soon as he said them. Her face softened, as if to relax her eyes for tears; her pointed cheekbones seemed to melt. She got up, picked up her fading camouflage backpack from under the coat rack, opened the door and walked out. She was so skinny that her clothes never quite fit her and that night they seemed even looser as she slipped through the door.

'Should I go after her?' I said, turning to face him. The fact that I was even asking meant that I didn't want to go. And I could tell from the way he placed the wooden salad bowl on the table that he didn't want to go after her either. It occurs to me now that I was stepping into her mother's inactive role, practising ambivalent parenting.

I had been parented much differently. My anxious migrant-worker parents took an interest in everything I did. They had only allowed me to hang out with the children of their ambulant colleagues, fellow captives, with whom I'd never really forged a bond. I suppose I could have tried to be a brilliant student and, like many of those kids, plotted my escape via an Ivy League education. But my unstable adolescent life had left me longing for so much that, had I not been accepted to the one college that had taken me, I would have joined the army.

Even now, I try not to make a big deal about it, but Polly's father – in my own version of partial erasure, no longer my college philosophy professor but Polly's father – was the first man I ever had sex with. This was something he seemed so proud of that I was afraid he would blurt it out in the two back-to-back classes I took with him my first year of college.

'One of the last virgins in the world,' he would occasionally whisper in my ear, 'and I had her.'

One of the millions of asses in the world, I would think, and I love him.

After an evening at his apartment, I would feel guilty when I returned to the room I shared with Polly. Each moment with him felt like something I had stolen from her. I would be dying to tell her what we had just done, substituting another name for his, but in the end I decided to lie, telling her I'd been at the library, studying for exams I was failing because of my borderline obsession with my own body and these new sensations I was feeling.

'Do you have a phone number for Polly?' I asked, after he had been silent for a while. So silent that I feared he had fallen asleep.

'Her phone is now disconnected,' he said.

He didn't know this, but Polly had learned about Kenbe, the Haiti women's group, from me. I had gone to the Global Experience office and had picked up a small, matt fold-out brochure and had brought it back to the room with me. She had taken it from my desk and had slept with it on her chest that night and many nights after that. How ironic it would have been for me, I thought, to have tried everything possible to escape my parents in rural Georgia only to end up farther from them physically but even closer to their past in Haiti. But their country, the one they had lived in and had left with me as a baby, cradled in their arms, and the country I would now see, the one in the brochure, would not be the same. That country would have long days of consoling wounded women and rocking the enormous heads of their hydrocephalus-stricken offspring and preemies that would barely fit in the palms of my hands. My parents' country would still be green and beautiful, just as they'd vaguely described it to me now and then. Their country would have no need for people like Polly and me to interrupt our lives to go and help.

In the end I didn't volunteer. Instead I spent my spring break working extra hours at the cash register at Whole Foods. I had relieved myself of any guilt by clinging to the possibility of the last line in the brochure, that one did not need to volunteer only during spring break, but could do it at any time.

Sherlon had fallen asleep. I could hear him snoring loudly on the other end of the line.

'Sherlon,' I shouted his name several times, but he did not answer. Is this what it was like, I wondered, to be his daughter?

I was about to hang up the phone when I heard him mumble my name.

'Clio,' he said, 'do you know where my daughter is?'

I did, but I wasn't sure I was ready to tell him.

The walls of the Kenbe office in Miami's Little Haiti neighbourhood were covered with photographs of sad but hopeful-looking women, their eyes aimed like laser beams at the camera which had hoped to capture their image, to elicit pity and sympathy. Unlike the Haitian restaurant and barbershop next door, which blasted lively music from giant speakers into the street and had people walking in and out, the two-room Kenbe office, though it was completely visible from the street, was quiet, and you could see Polly and another woman in profile as they worked at their desk. Even in the eighty-degree-plus heat, Polly was wearing a thick brown velvet jacket that looked at least thirty years old. She had probably picked it up from one of the many Salvation Army and Goodwill thrift stores that provided most of her wardrobe. Her face was even more gaunt now than when I had last seen her and she was stooped over, reading files through a fragile-looking wiry pair of glasses.

I watched her for a long time from a wobbly table outside the coffee shop across the street. She spent hours staring at her computer screen and only occasionally stopped to file a few pieces of paper in what seemed like small filing cabinets beneath the desk. A while ago, I had suspected that she might be here, based on the way she had carried the Kenbe brochure around for days. She wasn't there that day, but the woman at the other desk, her boss, had told me that she would be back in a couple of hours. I had left and never returned.

Finally, Polly got up, strolled over to the other woman's corner desk, exchanged a few words, then walked to the front door and out on to the street. She walked down the short block, keeping her eyes on the sidewalk as if searching for something. Moving closer to the kerb, in between some parked cars, she picked up some cigarette butts and, after sorting them, packed the rest into her pocket, cupped her hands around her mouth and lit one. She had not been a smoker when we were room-mates, but then again she might have been without my knowing it. Maybe she was one of those smokers who only smoked the remainders of other people's cigarettes. I finished my coffee and crossed the busy street, still hoping somehow that I could make our meeting seem accidental.

'Hey, Pol,' I said, when she looked up and saw me.

'Hey.' She opened one of her palms, spat in it and put out the stub with her spit then put it back in her pocket.

'What are you doing here?' she asked. She didn't sound angry, just surprised.

'So you went on the spring-break trip?' I asked.

She turned toward the window, the office and her desk and nodded. She had left one of the drawers on her small cabinet open and she suddenly seemed torn between going back in to close it and standing there to talk to me.

'How are you?' I asked.

Pointing to her flat chest, she said, 'Me?'

Accustomed to her delay tactics – avoiding eye contact and repeating questions – I repeated the question.

'I am fine,' she answered then.

I followed her gaze. She was watching a fox terrier, which was tied to a parking meter in front of the coffee shop across the street. The fox terrier was mostly white, with black patches, and it looked old. Or at least I thought she was watching the terrier. I remembered telling her how, soon after I had turned fifteen, I had convinced my parents to let me get a learner's permit. One day I was driving with my mother on a dirt road when a stray dog came out of nowhere. The window was down in the car because my mother was teaching me to drive the way she claimed people learned in Haiti, including how to signal with my hands. When the car hit the dog, I heard the crash then the long whimper. It was not exactly what I had expected a wounded dog to sound like. Maybe an eternal bark – the equivalent of a scream – even a barking at the sky, but not a pleading moan like the one my mother and I were both hearing coming out of the dog as the car was passing over it. I had pleaded with my mother to stop, but she'd refused, even as we looked back and saw the dog vainly try to stand up on one hind leg as the other three crumbled underneath it. There was no blood, which I found strange, but I wondered how long it would take that dog to die. And I wondered how long that image of the dying dog would remain a secret between my mother and me.

'I'm sorry,' I told Polly.

'Why?' she asked, still watching the dog.

'Because of your father,' I said.

'Come and have a coffee with me,' she said. She turned back to look at the open drawer and at the other woman in the office who was also watching us. The woman was a few decades older, maybe our mothers' age, but she was beautiful, eggplant-coloured with bright red fingernail polish, which neither of our mothers would wear. She waved at us and, jealously, I didn't wave back. Holding up one index finger, Polly pointed at me then at the coffee shop. The woman nodded her approval.

I felt like holding Polly's hand as we crossed the street and I would have, I think, if she weren't walking a whole lot faster than me. Neither one of us stopped when we passed the old terrier, which appeared listless on the hot sidewalk concrete. I followed Polly to a table in the back of the coffee shop, near the bathrooms. The air was cooler in that spot, but it was also dark and the aroma of cocoa and coffee was strongest there. A man came over and seemed both annoyed and disappointed when we only ordered two hot chocolates and none of the paninis and sandwiches and desserts he kept recommending.

Sitting there, it suddenly felt as though our time together had no limit, as if we might be silently sipping our hot chocolates forever.

'I'm not seeing your father any more,' I told her.

'Why not?' she asked, matter-of-fact, as though we were talking about someone who had been living in the dorm room across from ours.

'Because of you,' I wanted to say, but perhaps that was only a part of it. 'Because', I said, 'it was wrong.'

'Didn't my father teach you about moral relativism?' she said. 'Or did you ever even talk to each other?'

I thought she was about to throw the rest of her drink in my face and storm out, but we both sat there saying nothing as we calmly emptied our cups.

'Touché,' I said, 'and well deserved,' all the while marvelling at our relative calm and reserve. We were close to being adults now, both of us, no longer young women, almost real women.

'Have you been in touch with your parents?' I asked.

'No,' she said.

'Shouldn't you be?'

'Shouldn't you be?' She was mocking me.

She covered her face with her hands and rubbed so hard it seemed as though both her palms and her cheeks might be burning when she stopped.

'The spring-break trip was awful,' she said.

'So you went,' I said.

'It wasn't the trip itself that was awful,' she said. 'It was the circumstances.'

'How so?' I asked.

'I went to work at a rape crisis clinic, in a slum between a sewer ditch and a landfill, in one of the saddest places in the world,' she said. 'I saw women there who'd had their tongues bitten off by the men who had raped them.'

She saw girls, she said, eight, nine, who had vaginas as large as the top of the cup she had been drinking from, girls with syphilis scars running down their legs. She saw five-year-olds who had been raped by six or seven men, and saw mothers who took their thirteen-year-old daughters to tents where they sold them by the hour for sex while waiting to take them back home to give them a bath and comfort them and feed them the food that the survival sex money had just bought. These mothers would have offered themselves for the survival sex, except the men did not want them any more.

'People there,' she said, 'live so much of their lives on the edge. You walk into a cracked concrete building and you say to yourself, am I going to die? Then you see people sit on top of overloaded trucks going seventy, eighty miles an hour, accepting what we should all know, that life and death are beyond our control.'

I was the one who was now avoiding her eyes. I couldn't even look at the cups from which we had been drinking.

'Why didn't you go?' she asked.

Because I was afraid of exactly what she was talking about. I was afraid to see it. I was afraid to know it.

'But you are privileged now,' she said. 'You can give something.'

My parents had never talked about it, but my sense was that they had given everything. They gave everything so that I would never have to see this place Polly was talking about, experience it the way she had.

She had seen a few hopeful things though, she said, and when she came back, she had one of them tattooed on her chest, close to her heart so she wouldn't forget. Knowing her, I was afraid to ask what it was. I knew it would not be a tree, a beach, a hill, or mountain, a flower, or a butterfly.

One morning, she said, she woke up in the rape crisis clinic, where she was also living, and in the open window frame she saw clear plastic bags filled with water. The patients had strung them to the windows to keep out the flies. The flies and their many eyes, saw – it was believed – distorted, magnified reflections of themselves in the water and fled.

'How do you tattoo that on your chest?' I asked.

'The same way you tattoo a butterfly on your ass,' she said, raising her eyebrows to make sure that her point had hit home. 'But I had someone incompetent do it after I got back,' she added, 'and my tattoos look more like hot-air balloons than water bags.'

It was the first time I had seen her smile that afternoon. I reached for her hand as she started for the door, but she felt my fingers brush against hers and moved ahead. As she walked out, her back seemed a bit straighter than when she had walked in.

Outside, the old terrier at the parking meter was gone.

Standing where it had been, she said, 'My father would call my saying this redundant, but there is so much suffering in the world.'

'What do you do there?' I asked, pointing at her desk across the street.

'I recruit more volunteers,' she said.

'One day I'll have to go with you,' I said.

'If you can handle it,' she said.

'Can I come and see you again?' I asked.

'Sure,' she said.

Then she raised both her arms as if reaching for something above me. Her fingers landed on the back of my neck, clammy and shaking, nervous. They travelled up my neck toward my ears then over to my cheeks, even as her face was moving closer to mine. She smelled like chocolates and cigarettes and I didn't think I would, but I parted my lips when hers landed on top of mine and right there in the middle of the street, with puzzled people walking around us and staring, we kissed.

I was shaking and my head felt like it was on fire and for a moment it seemed as though she was trying to pour into my body, through her mouth, everything that she was feeling, everything she had ever felt, things that she had said and things that she could not say, things that she had done and could not do. I tried to keep us linked that way for as long as I could, clutching her back and inhaling her tongue, but then, pounding both her palms against my chest, she pushed me away.

The rest of the world was there again. I still felt feverish and naked, as she turned around and calmly walked across the street. I watched her go through the office door, sit down at her desk and turn on her computer. She turned her chair away from the street and said something to the other woman in the office and they laughed, a necks pulled back, mouths open to the sky type of laughter. I waited for her to look back and wave goodbye to me. She never did. ∎

GRANTA

UN-POSSIBLE RETOUR

Clarisse d'Arcimoles

WITH AN INTRODUCTION BY TÉA OBREHT

If I Could, I Surely Would

The man in my life is, at best, uncooperative when it comes to posing for photographs. Our holiday albums are littered with images of his tongue, his teeth, the whites of his eyes, blurry triplicates of him that remain undetectable until long after the actual moment of picture-taking. When I ask him why he does it, he is adamant: 'I don't need the picture,' he says, 'I have the memory.'

The first time he said this, it was a revelation. Don't the memory and the photograph go hand in hand? How can you revisit a memory without access to some accompanying picture? More importantly, how can others – those not fortunate enough to witness the more spectacular moments in your life, such as moose sightings or inspired teenage costuming – share in the memory without visual aids? But then I begin thinking about all those unknown-picture stories, the ones that circle around the mysterious uncaptioned photograph, the universally seductive ring of 'Who is the woman in the picture?' And it occurs to me that perhaps my boyfriend might be right. Perhaps the relic of a life is not the visual residue, but the memory itself. We are, after all, always chasing: our own ever-changing recollections and reminiscences, so that we can understand ourselves; the memories of others, to which we can never really connect, because no matter how detailed a story, no matter how accurate the picture, we can only understand the significance of a moment in someone else's life through the scrim of self-reflection.

The moment I see Clarisse d'Arcimoles's *Un-Possible Retour*, it confirms my belief that the universal exists in particularity. Her memories are present in this photo essay. Yet, when I see her photographs, I think only of my own memories, and understand more than ever that the people in my life who are constant, though they have been reshaped moment to moment by experience, by a thousand unsaid things that can never be summed up in a single frame, are not the same people now as they were in pictures fifteen years ago. I am reminded, too, of that near-inconceivable fact: that they were entirely different people, lives half-lived already, before I was even born; that by the time she was my age, my mother had already conceived me; that my grandmother had once summoned the courage to leave home and become a receptionist, the job that eventually united her with my grandfather.

I don't know what the moments recorded here mean to Clarisse d'Arcimoles; don't know a thing about her memories, except that the barest glimmer of them makes me want to hold on to my own.

If my interests lay elsewhere, if I were not still mourning the loss of my grandfather, I would probably be able to focus on how *Un-Possible Retour* subverts reality in the staged second half of each sequence, and perhaps question the notion of basing images on original, irreproducible memories. But, almost five years after his death, I still miss the man who all but raised me, teller of stories and believer of dreams, who perhaps more than anyone is responsible for the kind of woman I am today, and the last image of the sequence hits me like a gut-shot. ∎

Contact Sheet (My mother)
2009

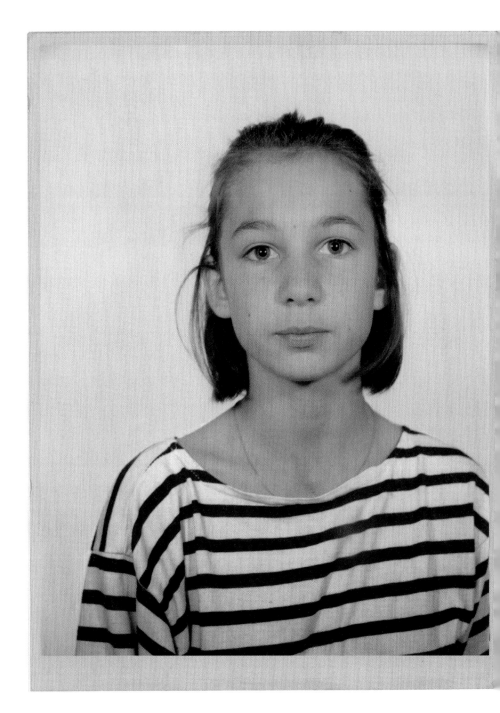

Camille (My sister)
2010

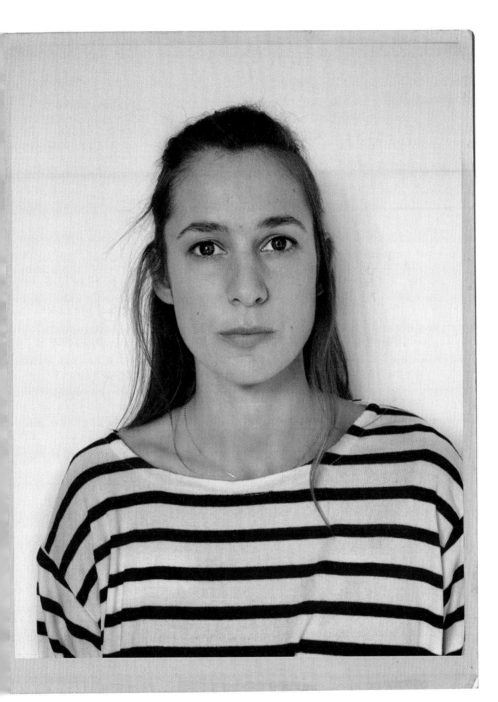

Religieuse (Self-portrait)
2009

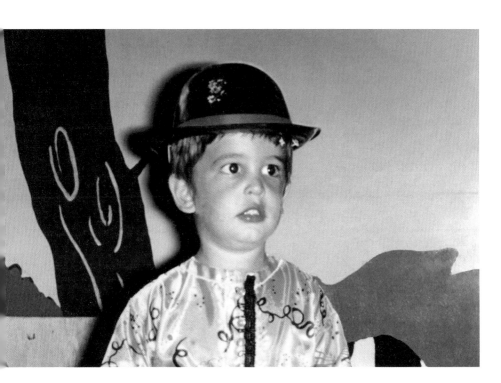

Carnaval (My brother)
2009

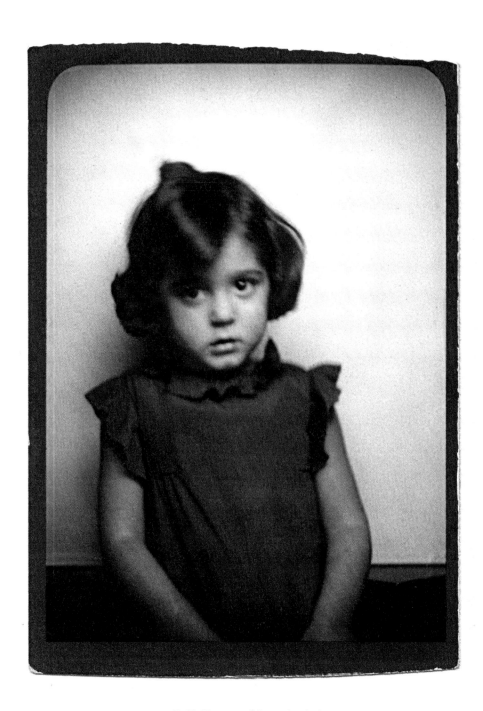

Naddy Photomaton (My grandmother)

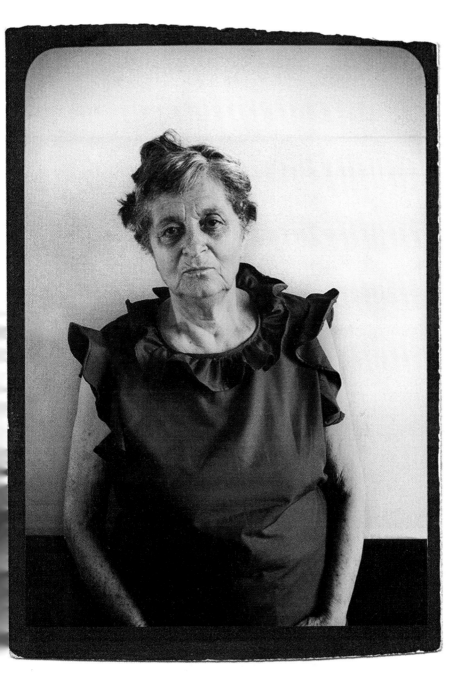

Legos (Self-portrait)
2009

Petit roi (My brother)
2009

Dad
2009

In the bath (Mother and sister)
2009

Daddy (Grandfather)
2009

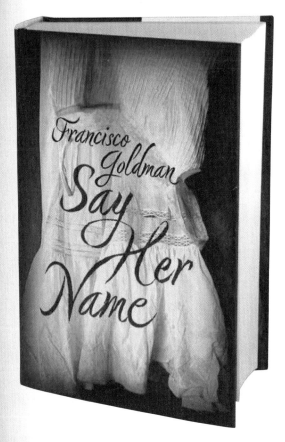

GRANTA

THE MAGAZINE OF NEW WRITING

SUBSCRIPTION FORM FOR USA, CANADA AND LATIN AMERICA

Yes, I would like to take out a subscription to *Granta*.

GUARANTEE: If I am ever dissatisfied with my *Granta* subscription, I will simply notify you, and you will send me a complete refund or credit my credit card, as applicable, for all un-mailed issues.

YOUR DETAILS

MR / MISS / MRS / DR ....
NAME ....
ADDRESS ....
CITY .... STATE ....
ZIP CODE .... COUNTRY ....
EMAIL ....
(Only provide your email if you are happy for Granta to communicate with you this way)

☐ Please check this box if you do not wish to receive special offers from *Granta*

☐ Please check this box if you do not wish to receive offers from organizations selected by *Granta*

YOUR PAYMENT DETAILS

1 year subscription: ☐ USA: $45.99 ☐ Canada: $57.99 ☐ Latin America: $65.99

3 year subscription: ☐ USA: $112.50 ☐ Canada: $148.50 ☐ Latin America: $172.50

Enclosed is my check for $_____ made payable to *Granta*.

Please charge my: ☐ Visa ☐ Mastercard ☐ Amex

Card No. ☐☐☐☐☐☐☐☐☐☐☐☐☐☐☐☐

Exp. ☐☐☐☐

Security Code ☐☐☐☐☐☐☐

SIGNATURE .... DATE ....

Please mail this order form with your payment instructions to:

Granta Publications
PO Box 359
Congers NY 10920-0359

Or call toll free 1-866-438-6150
Or visit GRANTA.COM for details

Source code: BUS115PM

MONA'S STORY

Urvashi Butalia

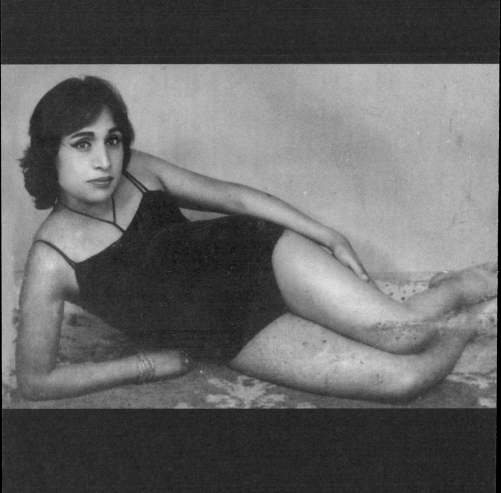

I first met Mona at a birthday party in a graveyard. That proximity of birth and death has stayed with us through the many years of our friendship. The back wall of her home abutted that of the morgue of a local hospital and Mona would often say to unsuspecting visitors – knowing full well the possible impact of her words – 'I have the dead behind me and the dead beneath me.' Then she might point to the graves on top of which people had built houses and add: 'It's a good way to live.'

At the time of that first meeting, I was looking for unusual stories about the Partition of India for a book I was researching. Friends suggested I talk to Mona and offered to take me to meet her. More than a decade has now passed since we met and got to know each other and, looking back, I sometimes wonder what either of us wanted from this unlikely friendship which crossed the barriers of class and gender in curious ways. I'm not sure I am any closer to understanding what, if anything, we've gained.

It was the 26th of January in Delhi, a crisp, clear, spicy-radish-and-tomatoes-in-the-sun winter morning that makes you glad to be alive. On this date, some fifty years ago, India had become a republic. Mona had chosen the anniversary to celebrate the birthday of her adopted daughter Ayesha; it pleased her that Ayesha had come into her arms precisely on the 26th of January. She would be free, like India.

The route to the graveyard, the walls of its compound, the pillars at its gate, were plastered with posters inviting all and sundry to the party; it was certainly the most unusual invitation I'd ever seen. Beside a somewhat makeshift, unfinished structure stood a wall about five feet high, and behind it men and women cooked food in large vats. *Pakodas* were being fried, their delicious aroma wafting out along the clear morning air, vying with the mouth-watering smell of meat curry and hot, oven-baked *rotis*. At one end of the compound, next to a cluster of graves, two people were busy chopping bananas, guavas and oranges into a spicy fruit *chaat*. Mona, large and imposing, hennaed and cropped hair spiking every which way, teeth stained with *paan*, her dark skin catching the winter sun, walked among her guests, offering food to one, a cold drink to another. But something was amiss. She didn't seem dressed for a party; her clothes were rumpled and somewhat grimy, her hair dishevelled. She looked distracted and unhappy – and there was no sign of her child.

It turned out that Ayesha hadn't come to her own birthday party because a few days earlier – or possibly it was some weeks – she'd been abducted. Or so Mona said. 'Abducted' is perhaps an odd word to describe what had happened to Ayesha, but she had indeed been taken away, by her adoptive 'grandmother', Chaman, and 'mother', Nargis, who – along with Mona – had formed themselves into a family for the child. Mona was devastated. She'd known of Ayesha's 'abduction' before she'd planned the party – after all, they had all lived together. But she'd gone ahead anyway, in the hope that making the party a public event would shame Ayesha's grandmother and mother into returning the girl to Mona's care. This didn't happen, but all the guests arrived nonetheless, and Mona was torn between her duties as a hostess and her concern over Ayesha's non-appearance. At some point Mona lay down in front of a small storeroom, defeated, but still insisting that Ayesha would come. 'I know she will,' she said. 'They're sure to bring her, it's her birthday.' But it was clear that her heart wasn't in it.

M y friends and I stayed on at the party for a while, although I don't think I realized then exactly how broken Mona was by her daughter's absence. I was fascinated by what I saw around me. Mehendiyan, the large, bustling compound in the heart of Delhi, held two graveyards for Muslims and was also the headquarters of a religious sect called Jamia Rahimia. Local lore had it that the founders of the sect had moved to Delhi from Persia in the nineteenth century, setting up in Mehendiyan, living, dying and being buried there. Then, in the absence of a successor to their leader, the sect disbanded, and some years later, squatters began to move in, some of whom 'recreated' the sect to give themselves legitimate access to the land. The compound housed two mosques and a school for the religious instruction of young boys, the buildings set apart from the graveyard. Somewhere deep inside its portals was the small editorial office of an Urdu newspaper that had been, until recently, written by hand and then printed at a small offset press nearby.

Mona had built her home – or had begun to build it, for it was quite unfinished – to encompass a very small living area above several graves in which she said her ancestors were buried, on land that apparently belonged to her family. The structure consisted of a large wall covered with shiny white bathroom tiles featuring pictures of the Taj Mahal, forming a semicircle around what appeared to be a water tank sunk into the ground. At one end stood two other unfinished and free-standing walls, built of trellised brickwork, and between them a door that led to a small storeroom. This was where Mona said she slept.

Most of the guests at the party were male, though there were women as well. These were Mona's friends and neighbours, some of whom lived in the old city of Delhi nearby. Mona talked to everyone. Speaking to the men she became, or assumed, the male persona of Ahmed-*bhai*, and many of the men present addressed her as such. Speaking with the women she was Mona, or *baji*, or *behen* – all female terms. This quick switch from one identity to the other, and the ease with which she achieved this, was remarkable. Now she was Ahmed and now *baji* or Mona, and no one seemed to find this odd.

At some point, mindful of my reason for visiting her, Mona found a half-hour to take me aside and talk to me about Partition. I filled several pages with her stories and some of these later appeared in my book. My friends and I left after spending several hours with Mona that day. The party had continued without Ayesha and after a while no one mentioned the child. There was food to be eaten and conversations to be had and people to be entertained, so all this went on until dusk set in and the crowds began to dwindle. I spent some time that night writing my notes on the experience and then put it out of my head. A few weeks later, Mona called. Was I a writer? she wanted to know. Why didn't I write her life? There was so little people knew about the way *hijras* lived, and she would give me all this information. Come and see me, she said, and we'll talk.

II

And so we began. My initial visits were tentative, hesitant, unsure. Then she suggested we fix a regular slot and Sunday afternoon became our time. I would drive across to see her in her graveyard compound – where I soon became known as the woman with the red car – and shortly after I arrived, she would shoo away all her hangers-on. She would talk and I'd write detailed notes. It wasn't long, though, before the note-taking stopped and our conversation becaome more personal. We began to talk, not as researcher and researched, but as two women would. She was curious about me – why was I not married? What did it mean to be a feminist? And I was curious about her – what was it that so attracted her about femaleness? Had she really wanted to be a woman so badly that she was willing to give up everything – home, family, friends – for it? Over time I became her friend, confidante, banker (for those times when she found herself broke and needed money), adviser and, I discovered one day, a sort of 'ticket' to respectability. I'd once told her that I had been invited to dinner (along with about two hundred others, but this she conveniently forgot) by Sonia Gandhi, and I found that she had announced to her neighbours that I 'regularly' dined with the most powerful woman in India! Her questions, and her actions, never ceased to surprise me. One hot summer afternoon I arrived to find her sitting large and naked on a *charpai*, a string cot, with a bucket of water at her feet. She was preparing to bathe. 'Don't be embarrassed,' she said to me, seeing the look on my face. 'We're all women here –

I've nothing that you don't have,' she said, pointing to different parts of her anatomy and grinning at my discomfiture. Gradually, this too would disappear. As would my fear – and I'm ashamed to say it, but I was fearful – of being in a largely poor and Muslim (and as I then imagined, hostile) place. Over time, the mullahs, the young boys in skullcaps, the battery operators, the knife sharpeners and rickshaw pullers and the gravedigger who occupied the compound all became my friends, familiar, sometimes funny, often lonely men, a number of them joining Mona in the quest for femaleness.

III

Mona Ahmed was born a boy, the third child after two girls, in 1937. In the narrow, congested streets of Ballimaran in Old Delhi, where her father ran a small business selling skullcaps, the birth was greeted with joy. The family could no longer be dismissed – they now had a boy to continue the line. But things didn't quite turn out as expected.

'From the moment I became conscious of myself as a person,' she says, 'I felt I was a misfit. I was convinced I had been born in the wrong body. I really wanted to be a girl.' It wasn't only the physical fact of her maleness that made her uncomfortable, but also the cultural baggage that accompanied it. She liked dolls and 'feminine' things, preferred girls as friends. This made her the butt of many jokes at school, as well as a source of anxiety for her parents. She was a lonely child, an outcast among boys who saw her as effeminate yet unable to join the girls because the society in which she lived was conservative: there was no space for girls and boys to play together. Often, she would leave home for school but instead spend the day sitting in the park, alone. It was not until much later in life that she would find what she believed was a place for herself.

'When I was around ten, in 1947, my family moved to Pakistan,' she says. 'Later we came back here. I was unable to get admission to a school, and my parents were quite concerned about my girlishness –

so the *maulana* was brought in to teach me. He would read the Quran to me.

'One day, the *maulana* molested me. I remember the terrible pain. I was bleeding and hurting. I told my mother, who told my grandmother, and later they told my father. Then my grandmother and father, they beat up the *maulana*. At first he admitted he had done this and later he swore he had not. So my father punished me by sending me back to him. I hated it – I was frightened of him. My mother fought with my father about this, but he refused to change, he was adamant. He insisted the fault was mine.'

Mona was sent back to school, but nothing changed. She only ever had female friends, and she would play female roles in plays at school. The boys and the older men in her neighbourhood teased her, making her the object of their lewd jokes; people would say to her: '*Apa hai, bhai nahin hai*' ('She's a sister, not a brother').

Mona was eighteen when she first met the *hijras* who would change her life. In the time-honoured tradition, a group of them had come to a nearby home to bless a newborn child and sing and dance in exchange for money. Mona felt an immediate shock of recognition. 'These are my people,' she thought. 'Men who want to become women.' She followed them to a local tea stall and struck up a conversation. They recognized a kindred spirit. Several meetings later, after a particularly traumatic encounter with her father, Mona went to them in desperation and they offered her an escape. 'Come with us,' they said. 'We'll help you.' Mona didn't hesitate. Tempted by the *hijras*' promise of a nearly female identity, Mona left home and travelled to Bombay, where she lived with the troupe and prepared for her castration, a procedure known in the *hijra* community as 'nirvana'. 'I didn't actually need much preparation,' she told me. 'I'd already decided. I hated all those male genitalia.' She used the little money she had, the *hijras* helped out with the rest. 'They look after their own,' she said. Mona's penis and testicles were removed in a back-room surgery in

Belapur, a small village near Bombay. At the time, in the late fifties, sexual reassignment surgery was illegal in India, and unregulated. In Mona's case the local anaesthetic did not work very well and the pain was agonizing.

'Afterwards I felt an enormous sense of liberation,' she says. 'But at the time all I could think of was the pain.' Much later, Mona would tell me that although she'd always wanted to be female, she had not been prepared for the finality of castration. 'Suddenly, I realized that I had crossed the point of no return. There was now no going back.'

But Mona did go back – although unwillingly; the real point of no return was to come later. Her parents managed to trace her through a friend, who was then dispatched to bring her back from Belapur. 'I stayed at his home in Delhi until my wounds healed, and then I returned to my parents' home. But things did not improve – my father hated the idea of my effeminacy and continued to ill-treat me, so I did not tell him about the operation. But he would call me *hij* for *hijra*, and he would often say it would be better if I were dead. One night he even tried to strangle me. Then my brother-in-law came and took me away, and I stayed with him and his family for a while. But everywhere, things were difficult. I decided to go back to the *hijras*. My father protested, but the other people in my family said, "Let him go." Maybe they knew about the castration. Anyway, I left.'

IV

In the early days, Mona was happy with the *hijras*. She was treated well and taught to sing and dance, skills that would become her route to earning money. 'It was a wonderful life,' Mona told me. 'We'd dress up in nice clothes, go out to sing, dance or offer blessings.' But the community's rules were strict. Their earnings had to be handed over to the guru, the head of the society, and he'd share them among the troupe. She felt increasingly that she had landed among her own kind, that her sexuality and gender were finally not in question. 'I thought I'd found a home.'

But new homes are not so easily found, nor old ones left behind. Despite the violence and insults she had endured from her family, Mona's connection to them remained strong. She refused to give them up, worrying about her sisters and later even offering to pay for their children's education. For this, she was punished: in the *hijra* community, you do not live by the rules of 'ordinary' society. Once you've been inducted, family connections are to be severed, and loyalty to the guru must be absolute. Disobedience, resistance, even questioning, are often punished with violence, or – worse – ostracism. Mona had indeed questioned the guru, Chaman – a legendary figure in the streets of Old Delhi. She flouted his instructions about not keeping in touch with her family. She would phone, send money at festivals, fund her nephews' and niece's schooling. (She drew the line, however, at visiting them too often. Only when her father lay dying was she given permission to visit.)

There was another reason Chaman was reluctant to let Mona maintain contact with her family: every time she returned home, Mona switched identities, put on male attire – dull or dark-coloured *shalwar kurtas*, loose trousers with a long shirt that effectively hid her silicone breasts. (One of the first *hijras* to undergo a full sex-change operation – which is today routine for many – Mona had acquired her breasts and a vagina, as well as undergoing other surgeries, a few years after the castration.) For Chaman and Mona's fellow *hijras*, such ambivalence about identity was simply not allowed: you either were or were not part of the community. As Mona describes it: 'It's like being in a nunnery – the community is your family, and you dare not go out of it.'

Mona also desperately wanted something else, and here, for some reason, Chaman indulged her – up to a point. She wanted to be a mother. 'Why', she wondered once when I asked her about her longing, 'do people think motherhood can only be biological?' Mona yearned to experience motherhood – it was the only way for a woman to be complete, she said – so she begged Chaman to allow her to adopt a child. By now part of a communal household in old Delhi with Chaman as patriarch, Mona felt they had a home to offer the child she so wanted. As it happened, the *hijras'* neighbour died in childbirth, and her widower was reluctant to keep the child – a girl. Mona, Chaman and Nargis, another of Chaman's followers, took the child in, forming a family with Chaman becoming *Dadi* ('Grandmother' – although Chaman was always only referred to as 'he'); Mona was *Abbu* ('Father', although by this time she had become physically female), and Nargis became *Ammi* ('Mother').

The real role of mother was played by Mona, however. She visited paediatricians and midwives to learn how to hold, burp, wash, care for and bring up a child. Until the age of six – the birthday celebrated at the graveyard – Ayesha was raised by Mona. But Chaman grew jealous of the growing affection between Mona and the girl, and critical. His authority was being undermined, his instructions flouted. Mona listened to doctors, to 'normal' people, not to him, and the child and mother seemed to share a bond that effectively left him out. He decided to separate them. With his customary authority, Chaman took Ayesha away from Mona. Fierce in her attachment, Mona fought hard to retain the child, but she did not succeed.

With Ayesha now in his control, Chaman shut down the communal home, moved his flock to a new location and barred Mona from joining them. Desperate and despairing, Mona began to drink, squandering everything she had on cheap liquor. 'I would often wake up in some sleazy street,' she says, 'and find myself next to other drunks – beggars, thieves, rickshaw pullers.' When liquor did not work she turned to religion, at first praying five times a day and then going on the hajj. When she came back, as the male-identified hajji Ahmed, people greeted her with flowers and sweets – but Chaman did not appear, nor did Ayesha. Only when she committed the cardinal sin of going to the police to complain about Chaman having thrown her out, thus grossly violating the rules of the *hijra* community, was she ostracized. She couldn't take part in any communal activity, and with the singing and dancing now not an option for her, her earnings were drastically reduced. As with everything else she fought this verdict too, trying to regain her place in *hijra* society, but she found no support. Chaman had ensured that the entire 'council of elders' of the *hijra* community was on his side. And no one dared to go against the guru.

It took several years for Mona to accept the fact that Ayesha would not be returning to her, that there was no way for her to reclaim her child. Gradually her store of love and the desire for motherhood gave way to a sort of indifference. When I first began visiting Mona, Ayesha would figure often in our talks, and she would try to call the girl at Chaman's home using my phone so that Ayesha would not recognize the number and reject the call. Ayesha had strict instructions from Chaman that she was not to give in to Mona's pressure to see her. Mona later stopped trying to phone. Once she bought a second-hand computer, hoping to lure the child to her home, but to no avail. Then she just gave up.

V

As Mona and I became friends, we became more involved in each other's lives. She began to return my visits. One day, fed up with her own company, she arrived, resplendent in black and gold, at my office and demanded tea and biscuits. 'So this is what normal life is like,' she said, sitting across from me at my table, and I was immediately embarrassed by the 'normalcy' of my existence. A few years into our friendship, my father died and Mona turned up at my family home to offer her condolences. Dressed in the white of mourning, she sat and held my mother's hand, telling her that she too knew what it meant to be alone, without a man. Alone and without a man? The part about being alone I could understand, for much of the time she was actually alone, a stranger now to the *hijra* community. But without a man? I thought that was a strange statement from someone who had spent her life trying to be a woman. And yet, in some odd way, as I got to know Mona better, I realized that the hated male identity had not been abandoned after all, it lay there, somewhere deep down, to be called upon when some 'clout' or power was needed, or when a group of male visitors turned up bearing large bottles of rum and smuggled whisky. Schooled in the hard feminist politics of the street, I didn't quite know what to make of this. Ought I to see her as a man or a woman – and did I have to see her as one or the other, when she herself so often switched? 'But why do you find this so confusing?' she once asked me. 'I'm a woman, I've always wanted to be one, it's that simple.'

But she wasn't only that. Some days, at her home, I'd meet groups of young men – slicked-back hair, shiny, pointy shoes, skin-tight trousers and an almost elusive sense of femaleness. She introduced me to them – Jugnu, Chand, Ankit, Dharmendra – but it wasn't until I'd met them a few times that I began to understand what I was seeing: young men transitioning (if one can use that word) from maleness to femaleness. They'd come to Mona for advice and support. 'There's really no one else who can help us to understand,' they told me. 'That's why we come to *baji*.' Some of them had begun to take hormones and you could see their faces becoming smooth, their body hair starting to drop off. One of them even looked as if he was beginning to grow breasts. His friends teased him gently and, I thought, a shade enviously, about this. Another day, Mona stood waiting for me as I arrived at Mehendiyan. 'Let's go,' she said, lifting herself into my car and leaning forward to turn the air conditioner on full blast. 'Where?' I asked. She told me not to ask questions and directed me across the old iron bridge on the River Yamuna, to a part of Delhi called Seelampur. 'We're going to DART,' she said. DART turned out to be an NGO funded by the Delhi government whose main business was Aids prevention, and it sent out groups of young boys to places where men sought sexual partners, to distribute free condoms. But every Sunday afternoon, DART transformed into something else – a space where men and transsexuals and *hijras* came together to cross-dress, and sing and dance. I met a man in a sari who offered me a cup of tea and introduced himself as an engineer, working for a large corporation, married with two children. 'I come here most Sundays,' he said. 'My wife knows, and she thinks it's OK for me to express the female part of myself; it also helps us to be friends.' Another frequent visitor was an old man, slightly bent over and frail, a tattered *keffiyeh* wound round his head, who sold home-made biscuits in the streets of the old city. 'He's also a *hij*,' Mona told me. 'If you lift up his clothes you'll see.'

What was it with all these men wanting to be women, I wondered. Here I was, a woman who thinks of herself as empathetic and quite open, surrounded by men who were doing their best to switch over to 'my' side, and I felt out of place, as if *I* did not belong. I was reminded of a conversation I'd once had with an Australian friend of mine, a lesbian and a feminist, as she and I stood and watched some *hijras* dance at a women's conference. 'I hate all this,' she'd said to me. 'We've fought so long and hard to carve out a little space for ourselves in society, to be able to make our voices heard, and here are these men pretending to be women, and they've come and taken it over.' Until she said it in so many words, I hadn't actually thought of it like that. Instead, I'd been wondering about what the experience of maleness and femaleness meant for the Monas of this world and how someone like me could understand it. Typically, Mona had the answer. '*Arrey*,' she said, 'why do you worry so much about this? What is there to think? I'm human, you're human, I'm a woman but sometimes I can be a man – I don't like being one, but sometimes it's useful. And anyway, we have something more in common and that is that both you and I, we're bachelors.'

VI

Bachelors we both may have been, but that's where, I think, the similarity ended. Or perhaps not, for there's no doubt that we bonded together strongly as women – Mona's natural empathy and sense of belonging in the world of women led her to be caring and affectionate towards me. She would often show concern that I did not colour my hair for example, or that I worked too hard. But something deeper – I'm not sure what to call it, class perhaps? – kept us apart. I could never, for example, invite her with me to a restaurant for a cup of coffee. Not, I think, because I was ashamed of her, but more because I worried about how she would be treated – she was often unbathed, unkempt, loud, sometimes violent – the rules of social behaviour as 'normal' people know them were alien to her. She never came to my house when I had friends to visit and I did not ask her. Gradually, I came to realize that by offering me her life to write about, Mona had hoped that I would be instrumental in bringing about a change, that somehow people would see her as a 'normal' person and would give her her due. And I? Perhaps it was the fear of not being able to meet her expectations that kept me from writing the book about her. Or perhaps not. But at any rate, I never did write it.

Today, Mona is in her seventies. Her home in Mehendiyan has expanded as she has taken over more and more land there. But it gives her little comfort. Her retinue of hangers-on has seriously dwindled, and she spends much of her time lying on her bed, barely moving, except when it is necessary. She seldom bathes, and is often depressed. In a strange reversal of the old situation, Ayesha, now nearly twenty and married, comes now and again to visit her. Chaman no longer tries to stop her. He's ninety, and probably tired. But for Mona, the indifference is now too deep, the hurt too profound. Ayesha's visits bring her no joy. 'It's too late,' she tells me. 'Far too late.' I still visit Mona most Sundays; our conversations are desultory, she no longer talks about what it means to her to be a woman. 'I've cut all connections now,' she says, 'with my real family and with my *hijra* family. There's really nothing left to live for. I used to think the dead were only around me, but now I think they're inside me as well.' ∎

GENTLEMEN

Eudora Welty

HELENA ARDEN

To the Editors, *The New Yorker*

March 15, 1933

Gentlemen,

I suppose you'd be more interested in even a sleight-o'-hand trick than you'd be in an application for a position with your magazine, but as usual you can't have the thing you want most.

I am 23 years old, six weeks on the loose in N.Y. However, I was a New Yorker for a whole year in 1930–31 while attending advertising classes in Columbia's School of Business. Actually I am a southerner, from Mississippi, the nation's most backward state. Ramifications include Walter H. Page, who, unluckily for me, is no longer connected with Doubleday-Page, which is no longer Doubleday-Page, even. I have a BA ('29) from the University of Wisconsin, where I majored in English without a care in the world. For the last eighteen months I was languishing in my own office in a radio station in Jackson, Miss., writing continuities, dramas, mule feed advertisements, santa claus talks, and life insurance playlets; now I have given that up.

As to what I might do for you – I have seen an untoward amount of picture galleries and 15 cent movies lately, and could review them with my old prosperous detachment, I think; in fact, I recently coined a general word for Matisse's pictures after seeing his latest at the Marie Harriman: concubineapple. That shows you how my mind works – quick, and away from the point. I read simply voraciously, and can drum up an opinion afterwards.

Since I have bought an India print, and a large number of phonograph records from a Mr. Nussbaum who picks them up, and a Cezanne *Bathers* one inch long (that shows you I read e.e. cummings I hope),

I am anxious to have an apartment, not to mention a small portable phonograph. How I would like to work for you! A little paragraph each morning – a little paragraph each night, if you can't hire me from daylight to dark, although I would work like a slave. I can also draw like Mr. Thurber, in case he goes off the deep end. I have studied flower painting.

There is no telling where I may apply, if you turn me down; I realize this will not phase you, but consider my other alternative: the U of N.C. offers $12.00 to let me dance in Vachel Lindsay's *Congo*. I congo on. I rest my case, repeating that I am a hard worker.

Truly yours. ■

ZLATKA

Maja Hrgović

TRANSLATED FROM CROATIAN BY TOMISLAV KUZMANOVIĆ

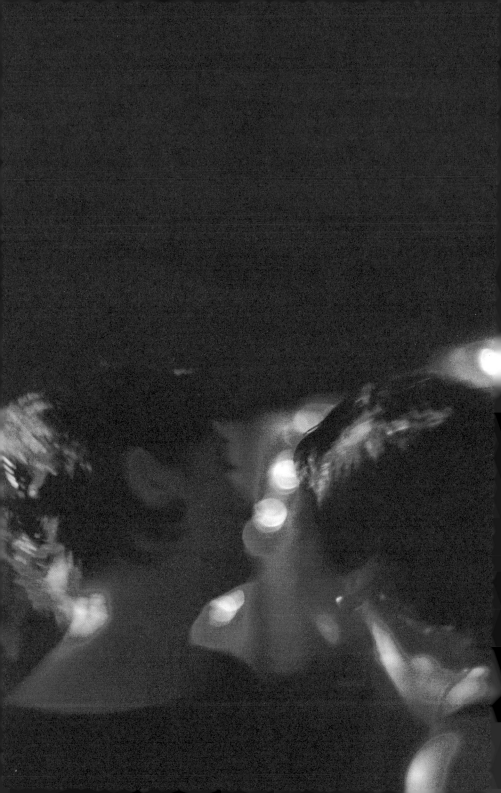

My head was hanging over the hair-washing basin, like a weighty pistil. With her soft, sensually slow circular movements Zlatka made her way through the wet mass all the way to the roots. Pleasure spread down my neck; I closed my eyes. Naturally, the tips of her fingers were seductively certain of their experience.

Later, she sat me in front of a large mirror. In it I caught sight of well-thought-through clips of scissors snipping at the split ends of my hair, and two creases incised into the corners of Zlatka's mouth as she said: 'I'll get that mane of yours in order.'

I lived near the train station in a neighbourhood built many decades ago for the families of railroad workers and machinists. Like tombstones over grave mounds, hardened chimneys rose from parallel rows of elongated one-storey buildings. Decaying, hideous buildings made of concrete, separated by narrow tracks of municipal ground and an occasional wild chestnut, shivered before sudden passes of express trains from Budapest and Venice.

My apartment perfectly blended with the sorrow of the neighbourhood; it grew out of it like a twig from a knarled old mulberry tree. I had two rooms at my disposal, but one smelled of damp so badly that I gave up on it. I slept, read and ate in the other larger room, in which I was – perhaps because of a red futon, the only new piece of furniture in the apartment – less often taken by the feeling that someone had recently died here. A large square window opened up on to yet another horrible one-storey building and let in just enough light to give me a sense of what I was missing. The cold crept in through the worm-eaten window frame and it made, as I breathed, the air evaporate from my nose in light little clouds. The space seemed impossible to warm. I sat next to the radiator, wrapped in a blanket.

Although I lived alone, I could feel the presence of others: every word of the neighbours' fights reached me through the porous walls, and in the evening when they made up and fucked, I could tell who'd come first by their muffled or piercing screams.

Through the poorly ventilated underpass, gleaming with neon signs and small shop windows, in gushes, unstoppable like viruses, working people and students hurried downtown. At the station at the entrance into the underpass the rattling buses that had brought them here from the suburbs gathered their strength for a new ride. Homeless people with their red noses dragged around with their plastic bottles and hauled their heavy stench behind them. Loudspeakers whined advertisements for prize contests, perfumes and meat-product sales in the supermarket on the basement level.

That winter life spun around in circles of drunkenness, hangover and sleep. Despite the no-crossing sign, I crossed the railroad next to the switchman's box. I pulled up the legs of my trousers so as not to get them dirty with the black grease that covered the rails – and jumped across looking left and right. I stayed at the Railroader's until closing. When I sloped home drunk, I paid less attention to the grime on the rails: after a few weeks in the new neighbourhood, the legs on all of my trousers were soiled with the black substance that wouldn't come off in the wash.

I met Zlatka on that day when DJ Scrap played at the Railroader's. I wanted to see the concert; not so much because I craved the Balkan Drum & Bass, but because I feared the loneliness that would have most certainly skinned me to the shuddering, sad core had I stayed home that evening, alone, with all those sober thoughts and the moans from the apartment next door.

Again there was no warm water. My hair had been greasy for days. I walked into the first hairdresser's salon I came across: it was actually a large glass kiosk. The salon was called Rin Tin Tin and it serviced both men and women at discount prices.

Zlatka was alone in the salon. When I entered, she crushed her cigarette against the side of the ashtray and put down the magazine she'd been leafing through. 'How can I help you?' she said. The beauty of her face – prominent cheekbones and large, dark eyes, her nose and lips, eyebrows, fringe, chin – did not fit the salon's interior. In the cabinet, which looked as if it had been stolen from a landfill, there were plastic boxes with curlers, scissors and shampoos, two little dried-up rose bouquets, a frame with the price list and a photo of a laughing dog. Faded posters of women with their puffed-up hairdos decorated the glass walls.

I was embarrassed because my hair was dirty and I felt sorry for Zlatka's fingers slowly making their way through my greasy curls under the stream of warm water. She told me I had split ends and they needed to be trimmed. I told her to go ahead and do it; prices were sensationally low anyhow.

An early, gentle winter evening at the Railroader's doesn't mean much: the light of day doesn't make its way through the windows obscured by painted canvases; sitting in booths always feels like being deep inside the catacombs. I twirled a lock of my hair, shiny and squeaky from washing, around my finger and let the waitress pour mulled wine from a large pot into my cup; she did it using a ladle as if serving soup. Behind my back, DJ Scrap was pushing a metal box from one end of a small stage to another, dragging the cables that came along with the box, and every now and then stopping by the microphone, tapping it lightly and saying: 'Check, check, one-two, one-two.'

Someone was throwing a birthday party; drinks started flowing faster, the atmosphere loosened slowly, sentences became funny and amusing. Someone complimented me on my hairdo. It was strange to take a compliment; perhaps I might have even blushed a little. Time rushed forward and when I glanced behind my back again the club was already full to the brim, strobe lights pierced the darkness and the voice of DJ Scrap, who had finally arranged all the props around the stage, confidently took hold of the microphone and released a salvo of loud kisses at the crowd. He promised them, in a thick Serbian accent: 'Tonight, we party!' And when the too loud music started, the groaning of admirers intensified together with uncontrollable flailing of limbs all over the dance floor. Soon the ventilation problem again made itself obvious: the passion of DJ Scrap's admirers condensed into drops of sweat, which gathered on the ceiling then and slimed down the windows.

I downed yet another shot that someone, when I wasn't looking, had placed in front of me.

She sprung out of the crowd and elbowed her way next to me at the bar. She waved at the waitress with a crumpled bill and yelled in a raspy voice: 'A beer! Large!' I recognized her immediately although now her hair was rowdy and her mascara beautifully smeared under her eyes. I couldn't take my eyes off her.

'Hey, ciao!' I howled in greeting, trying to out-shout the noise. She gazed at me as if she were nearsighted, but that lasted only a second; the next moment she offered me a wide smile, leaned towards me and in a cracked voice asked what I was drinking. I pointed at the steaming cauldron and she got me a cup of mulled wine and sat next to me. 'You're alone?' she asked and that was enough to start with, to fill the silence with trivialities. She was also alone; she'd come to the concert straight from work. She didn't care much about DJ Scrap, had never heard any of his songs, she just felt like going out. She told me there had been a competition on the radio and that she had made the call, gave the wrong answer to the prize question but had won two tickets anyhow. She couldn't get anyone to come out with her because it was the middle of the week, her friends had children, worked, didn't feel like it . . . she had almost given up. Still, she was glad she was here. By the way, her name was Zlatka. 'That's such a nice name,' I said, and it sounded sweeter than I wanted.

A dreadful guy in a leather jacket approached us when the fuse blew. There must have been a short or something; the lights went out, the music stopped, the crowd grew restless. The problem was solved in a couple of minutes, Scrap screamed into the microphone a little, fiddled with his cables and as soon as he found his bearings he again cranked up the volume to the max. Whipped by strobe lights, the dancers screamed gratefully.

As soon as the power came back, the guy in the leather jacket leaned over us; he wanted badly to stand at the bar right between Zlatka and me. He came to us from the back and put his arms around us as if wanting to share his deepest thoughts and fears with us. I took my drink and stepped away. I expected Zlatka to do the same.

But she didn't move. She let him sit next to her, on my stool, and she even moved closer to him. The greasy leather jacket was screening her from me. Still, I could see her smiling flirtatiously, enjoying his attention.

Standing alone behind her back, I felt rejected and insecure. I approached the edge of the dance floor and danced a bit holding my cup, then I downed it to get it out of my way and let the dancing crowd suck me in. In a moment I was jumping all over the place and screaming into my clenched fist meaningless chunks of verses that kept repeating over and over again as if the CD were skipping.

The hair on my forehead soon went limp from moisture. At the right moment, pushing her way through shirtless young dancers, Zlatka appeared in front of me with a smile on her face and two pints of beer in her hands.

'The DJ rocks!' she yelled into my ear and started coiling around me like a snake in some sort of a parody of a dance. It made me laugh. She swung her hair, flexed her neck to the rhythm of the music and at the end of every song screamed so much that the veins on her neck popped up and her cheeks reddened. Everything was good again, as if that guy had never happened.

The people around us were just a moving background, extras in a movie starring Zlatka and me. I got carried away. At moments I felt rapture, thick and saturated, clotting in me, somewhere in my lungs, in my oesophagus – I had to open my mouth wide and yell into the noise, anything, just to let it, this something, come out of me.

When some bouncy song started playing, the half-naked boys began jumping all over the place and pushed us on to each other. I grabbed her forearm, slippery from sweat. Then she kissed me on the cheek, just for the sake of it. She was smiling.

After the concert the crowd dispersed towards the toilet and the bar. The dive's regular musical repertoire was now in place; we stayed on the dance floor and danced a bit more and shuffled plastic cups with our feet.

'I hate it when the party finishes,' Zlatka said. She slurred words. 'I sober up immediately when they turn off the music and switch on the lights. And when I see these bottles and cups all over the place . . . it's like an apocalypse.'

I couldn't agree more. Everything is somehow more bearable in the dark.

When we got out, our bodies steamed. The cold forced us to hunch our necks into our shoulders like turkeys. We stood at the door and watched the darkness around us. In the distance, down the railroad, the train station glowed.

'What do you wanna do now?' she asked. I didn't feel like going home. The very thought that this night, so opulent and alive, could wither in the loneliness of my cold hole, on the stretched-out red futon to the background of the muffled squealing of the water heater, made me draw my neck into my shoulders even more. And I couldn't even imagine taking Zlatka there. 'OK, let's go to my place,' she said as if she could read my mind. She jangled her keys and pointed at the old, white Yugo parked at the entrance to the dive.

We took our time, played the game of delayed pleasure, which – it was clear the moment we had gotten in the car, the moment we had stepped into the elevator – was as imminent as sobering up.

The apartment was on the eighth floor of a high-rise in Sopot, a shady part of Novi Zagreb.

'It may be small, but the welcome is big.' Zlatka spouted the slogan for Daewoo Tico, the smallest of small cars, and let me in.

The hallway was also a kitchen; further ahead there was a larger room whose glass wall separated it from a narrow balcony with a concrete fence. We had to be quiet so as not to wake up Mila, her daughter, sleeping in the other room. Framed photos of Zlatka and her daughter smiled down from bookshelves. Not taking off my coat, I stepped out on the balcony to get some fresh air. I felt a little dizzy; the vista of concrete lumps wobbled in front of me. Deep down below my feet Dubrovnik Avenue was seething. The cars rushed maniacally through the traffic lights trying to catch the green. Behind me, back in the apartment, Zlatka put on a CD with covers of sixties hits. 'Why can't I stop and tell myself I'm wrong, I'm wrong, so wrong,' softly sang some woman, perhaps a black woman. Zlatka came up beside me.

'See that skyscraper?' She pointed her chin towards the building separated from ours by a concrete yard the size of a basketball court. 'Some woman fell from her balcony yesterday, from the eighth floor, just like this one, across the way. She leaned over and fell,' she said and gazed down into the darkness. 'I keep thinking about it. I wonder if she did it on purpose. I mean, these railings are quite high, you can't just fall over.'

I lowered my eyes into the abyss below. I imagined the police and the forensic team gathering around a fat housewife's corpse and a huge bloody stain that remained on the yard after the investigation.

'This morning I met a neighbour in the elevator and she told me a lot of the tenants didn't go to work yesterday so that they could see what was going on. They stood on their balconies as if they were in the stands somewhere; they spent the whole afternoon like that. Primitive bastards.'

'It's the same everywhere,' I said.

Down on the avenue a car ran the red light.

She offered me her toothbrush to brush my teeth. I showered with her shower gel, I put her lotion on my body and used her make-up remover and cotton pads to take off my make-up. When

I was done, she tossed me a pink T-shirt with Mickey Mouse's picture on it. We opened the couch, put on the sheets and turned off the light.

I started it. It was so natural to reach for Zlatka's breasts: it seemed they were shaped to fit the mould of my palms. My breasts are round in a perfectly expected kind of way; they're actually uninteresting. Hers are small, pyramid-shaped and soft. I cupped them, my eyes closed, not breathing, until her hardened nipples pressed against my palm. I kissed them gently. She held me tighter: I was hers. I kissed her neck and slipped under the sheet. I took off her panties. I paid attention to every movement of my head, to every twitch of her hips; I listened carefully to her breathing. She moaned. Just a short run of my tongue over her clitoris. She moaned again. Spread her legs wider, twisted and threw her head back.

It's morning, the blinds are up, the room is filled with light, and by my side Zlatka is still snoring like a man.

The first thing I see when I free myself from her embrace is the smiling face of a little girl, maybe ten years of age. Her brown hair reaches her shoulders, she kneels in front of me and her sleepy eyes are so close to mine I imagine that only a moment ago she must have kissed me or smelled me, like a dog. When I realize that it's Mila, she's already up, clanging cups in the kitchen, letting the water run in the sink, opening the cupboards.

'What tea do you like?' Mila asks me as she materializes before me again. Embarrassed, I sit up in the bed and immediately pain seizes at my temples. I feel stupid in the wrinkled Mickey Mouse T-shirt.

'Mint,' I say in a voice that this morning sounds squeaky and hoarse. I'm confused and slow. Anxiously I smile at Mila who, completely relaxed, begins to chatter about having an early music class, about her listening quiz. Her cheerfulness has a soothing effect; it makes me feel soft.

Mila puts the tea on the nightstand by my side of the bed and then shakes Zlatka's forearm. 'C'mon, Mom! I have an early class!'

And then she goes to the bathroom. Zlatka slowly opens her eyes and when she sees me, her face transforms into a lazy smile and then she buries her head in the pillow again.

'An early class,' she says and sighs, trying to get out of the bed. When she realizes she's completely naked under the comforter, she uses it to wrap herself up like a caterpillar. Without a word I reach for the stretched-out T-shirt she so resolutely took off last night and threw into the darkness of the room.

The school is nearby. During the short drive over the wet streets of Novi Zagreb I see a lot of right angles, heavy traffic, a few traffic lights, a tramline behind a neglected hedge. In a few minutes we are in front of a playground where a couple of boys are hanging around the basketball court, one of them holding a ball. Despite the cold, they have taken off their jackets and jump at each other, yelling. Mila adjusts her scarf and kisses Zlatka on the cheek; Zlatka kisses her on the forehead. 'Smart little forehead,' she says. I say, 'Good luck with your listening quiz!' Mila says, 'Thanks!' and leaves. We watch her as she runs, with a huge chequered bag on her back, towards a group of smiling girls; one of the girls waves at her widely, like the guy at the airport who signals to planes. They fall into each other's arms.

'They sit together in class,' Zlatka says, then puts the car in gear and we slowly move on.

The rest of our drive is more or less horrible. We feel Mila's absence and have nothing to replace it with. As if all that had happened last night had happened to other people. On the bridge, the line of cars moves more and more slowly. 'It's always like this in the morning, every morning,' says Zlatka. 'You simply can't avoid it.' Still, her fingers are restless on the wheel, and when she puts them on the gearshift, her fingertips leave a moist trace.

We move on in the pressing silence. Zlatka adjusts the heating, plays with the gearshift, looks down on the river the colour of chocolate pudding. I watch the cars stranded on the bridge. Today, they are mostly red.

She parks in front of Rin Tin Tin. I've told her she doesn't have to drive me all the way home, that I live really close, 'just around the corner'. Before we get out of the car, we sit there for a little while. We should say something; make our goodbye pleasant, normal. Still, we say nothing and everything is odd, unfinished, bumpy from insecurity. Then, as if synchronized, we reach for the doors at the same time and get out. A smile and 'Bye, see you!' and that's it. In a few steps Zlatka reaches the hair salon and disappears behind a glass door and a sticker saying, 'Push!'

I'm left alone.

Instead of going to my apartment, I head downtown across the railroad. At eight in the morning the city looks foreign enough that it seems it would be possible to get lost in it. I can't remember when I was last up this early. Everything is so interesting: teenagers with their colourful backpacks and bloated, down jackets running to catch the tram; women and men with circles under their eyes marching towards the escalators and glueing their sluggish eyes to the cover pages of the newspapers in the hands of a fat newsagent waving them about and yelling the headlines. A bit further, pensioners come out of the crowded tram carrying their canvas bags. Everywhere, the smell of coffee.

I let the traffic lights set my bearing: I go where they turn green. I walk along the botanical garden's fence; I glance at the sad, dried up puddle, which in May will become a small romantic lake. I walk over an asphalt strip of a grass-covered schoolyard, a path swelling over the chestnut roots. The school's cafeteria fills the morning with the smell of fried chicken – the smell of cooking oil floats all over the place, sticks against rusty waste bins and benches next to the further end of the hedge.

I walk into a coffee place on a small plaza. I've been here before and nod to a sinewy waiter with hairy arms who's fishing for dirty glasses in a foamy sink, sponging them vigorously. I say, 'Espresso, please,' and then take the wooden stairs to the first-floor gallery.

There's no one there. I sit by the window and watch: a flower shop, a kiosk, a hot-dog stand, a garbage man who's stopped his tricycle in front of a bakery to eat his bagel in peace. On the wall behind him someone has spray-painted 'IGOR' in red letters, with a frame around it and pierced with an arrow.

Then my eyes fall on a street clock. It stands above the monument of a war hero on the tips of his toes with a machine gun in his hand and a wince on his face. The hands read five to noon. But it can't be that late.

'Excuse me, what's the time?' I ask the waiter who's just brought me coffee. With his chin, he points to the clock on the wall across from me. It's just after nine.

I stare at the broken clock on the plaza and then at the brass soldier's face. That's my sign, it occurs to me, those arrested hands. I quickly finish my espresso, grab my scarf and my bag and then go downstairs, pay and leave. The garbage man's no longer in front of the bakery, he pedalled away. The sky is grey, the air sneakily cold, and the plaza livelier than before.

'It might snow,' I hear a woman say into her mobile. I pass by her, head back towards the botanical garden, towards the train station, I walk quickly, rushing. Trams, people, cars. Later I will remember nothing, not even the way I raised the legs of my trousers as I crossed the rails nor how I lost my breath at the switchman's box. I went on even faster because it was clearer to me than ever, than anything, that it was five to noon, it was high time – for anything.

At Rin Tin Tin, I saw through the window that there was no one but Zlatka. Trying to catch my breath, I watched her lean close to the mirror and trim her fringe using a small comb and scissors. She was so engrossed she didn't look out even once, and perhaps she didn't even blink. When she was done, she stepped away and blew her hair from her forehead. Then she disappeared behind a small door where the toilet had to be.

My heart was pounding in my ears as I fished for a lipstick at the bottom of my bag. I opened it and pressed it against the glass. My hands were shaking a little. My ears pounded. I hadn't planned it, the lipstick slid across the glass on its own: I wrote a large Z, shaky, the colour of a rotten cherry. It was as if I'd been freed from something. Then I wrote L-A-T-K-A. Zlatka. She was still behind that door. My breath was shallow and irregular. I had a little lipstick left. I drew a heart around her name and an arrow that pierced it. I put the lipstick back in the bag and went home.

I imagined her surprise as she approached the window, opened the door and ran her fingers across the grains of lipstick arrested in the letters. I imagined a smile rising in the corners of her mouth, making her face soft, those ray-like wrinkles around her eyes. This made me laugh as well, at first silently, warily, but then I couldn't take it any more: I shrieked and started laughing out loud. In front of a small store the drunks looked at me in wonder, frowning and squeezing the bottles in their hands. ■

WE'RE NOT IN THIS TOGETHER

Janice Galloway

Spring 1970

Sylvia fell halfway up a rope ladder and slid, almost soundlessly, on to the varnished hardwood floor. Miss McCourt rolled up her giant sleeves, lifted Sylvia like a baby and carried her through to the changing rooms. Some girls, the kind who genuinely believed that wall-bars were fun, didn't dwell. The rest of us turned. We watched Sylvia, borne away like the dead Ophelia in the teacher's arms, long hair trailing behind like an ash-blonde veil. Some swore they saw a smear of blood on her thigh; others, a flat dark stain on her knickers that refused to stay hidden. We watched till she disappeared through the elbowed-open space between the outside doors, chill gusting in to fill the place she had been. *That could be me next.* Nobody spoke out loud, but you could hear the words. They hung like drizzle in the air. One girl just kept walking across the high beam, her eyes focused on the path ahead. The rest of us stayed just where we were, listening. That could be me, the voices were saying. Any minute now, that could be me.

Next morning, it was. I woke up in a henna-coloured puddle and knew but said nothing, just went to wash. When I came out of the bathroom, Mum was stripping sheets. She took a KitKat out of her dressing-gown pocket and handed it to me without speaking. I ate it, wishing I could think of something to say. Mum snapped open a fresh top sheet.

Do you know what it is? she asked. I nodded. Right, she said. As long as you know. She smoothed the top sheet flat without looking up. I'll get you stuff this afternoon at Corner Duncan's. See and come home sharpish. That said, she handed me three pairs of school-issue navy bloomers and a paper hanky.

On you go, she said. You're not sick.

But she saw me off at the door. Padded like a hockey player,

I waved and felt tearful. I didn't feel good or clean or even defensible. I didn't feel right at all.

The front door was open when I came back at four, achy in places I couldn't pin down. Mum was waiting in the kitchen with a paper bag. She pulled out a cat's cradle of white-elastic strips with hooks attached and a white-mesh pad and started plying them together. The pad attached, she pushed her arms through the holes on either side of the hammock, pushed the belt around her elbows and paddled her arms to mimic legs.

See? she said. She paddled again. That's how you put it on.

She was mortified enough to be annoyed so I took the pieces she held out and didn't say thanks because it didn't seem to be a present.

Right, she said. Off you go. She thrust the new box of pads out for good measure and looked at me earnestly, ready to impart an important truth. Hide the packet under the cistern, OK? You don't leave things like that lying about. That's a rule.

OK, I said. I tried to look earnest. Confident now, she said I should get into bed when I was done and she'd fetch a cup of tea.

I didn't argue. Going to bed when she'd said herself I wasn't sick was confusing, but a drink in bed was a treat. I did what I was told, stripping out of my uniform, struggling into the stringy contraption she'd given me, and letting my nightie fall into place. She had chosen the orange brushed-nylon sheets when I went back through. They sparkled with static and smelled of fresh. I got hot Ribena, a handful of Jaffa Cakes, this week's *Bunty for Girls*, a leaflet and a couple of aspirin in foil as a reward for being cooperative. She looked relieved.

There, she said. She pulled a loose thread off the valance and settled it back in place again. All set. At least you don't have the bike any more. White saddle and everything.

I said nothing.

And don't go using the pads up all at once. It's me that pays for them. She stood, sighed in a way that suggested a job well done. Do you need anything?

I didn't, so she slipped back out to make my sister Cora's tea.

Thanks, I said as she pulled the door behind her. Thanks were in order. This was special treatment. I clutched the *Bunty* like a good-luck card then sank back into the pillow to read. *The Four Marys* – one ugly, one bright, one beautiful and one sporty – were being harassed by posh identical twins. You knew they were posh because they said *utterly beastly* all the time. An important match-winning hockey stick had been broken and nobody knew how it had happened. Suspicion fell on the twins but there was no proof. The girls had to uncover the twins' wickedness but didn't know how. *More next week.* My guts were starting to churn. I kept reading. *Wee Slavey (the maid with the Heart of Gold)* was in trouble for a suspected theft of a candlestick and had to catch the true criminal all by herself to escape being taken away by the police. She got no credit because she shouldn't have been out of the servants' quarters at that time of night. So the cook said she'd solved the mystery instead. Wee Slavey got more pots to wash and smiled through her tears. I had a bash at a story about an orphaned swimmer but it was no good. The stories seemed slight today, too ethereal away to trust. The black-and-white drawings were starting to spangle. They weren't girls after all, just drawings. And, today at least, drawings to fool somebody younger than me.

Bunty was cast aside for a crack at the leaflet. It was printed on shiny Izal-type paper with two line drawings and densely packed, spidery words. Periods went on for days, it seemed. At the top, a drawing of half a leg with some mushroom-like bulbous tubes was supposed to show you why. The words said this was growing up and would happen every twenty-eight days from now on, regular as clockwork and probably forever. I rubbed my eyes, rested back on the pillow and heard the door click, and felt the rush of cold air that meant Cora was home from work.

Coo-ee, she said, perky. Out there in her world, it had clearly been a good day. My mother's greeting was lost in a low burr of mumbles and I knew she was giving away my secrets. Right on cue, my sister called from the hallway.

Hoo, she said. Her voice was cheerful as cherry cake. The game's afoot! I imagined her rubbing her hands. Here comes trouble.

The TV button clanked and the sound came up, crackling. I heard the nylon lining of her coat shivering off her shoulders, the metallic scrape as she hung it in the hall cupboard and dusted herself down.

Welcome to the bloody club, she shouted. Then she laughed in her throat, thick and hearty. It's all fun and games from here, chum, you mark my words. It'll be boys next. Wait and see. You'll be chasing bloody *boys*.

What boys had to do with periods was beyond me. There hadn't been one mention of them in the leaflet, and it should know. It was just Cora being a pig as usual. The dragging pain beneath my belly advanced as I curled into the covers, hiding. Already, Cora was being pass-remarkable about the news headlines and yelling for her tea. I was in bed, it seemed, for the foreseeable. I swallowed the aspirin still there on the bedside cabinet, coughed, then stared out of the window at Mr Gregg's pigeons till they started staring back.

The McFarlanes' TV bellowed as they switched it on, then fell back to a low mutter. Ours promised *a bright weekend ahead* before Cora switched channels, singing 'Delilah' in a jokey voice, which probably meant Tom Jones was on later. Mum roared to ask if she wanted a fried egg. My coloured pencils were in the living room and *Bunty*'s stupid face was grinning from the bottom of the bedspread. Annoyed, I kicked her off and pulled the covers over my head, sparking brushed-nylon shocks all the way down to my bones. Pigeons were crooning. Captain Birdseye was extolling the virtues of fish fingers. Avon called and Ariel with enzymes digested the stains other powders left behind. Mum shouted did I want to eat yet but I didn't answer. I was holding my breath, refusing, point-blank, to cry.

Spring 1973

In Largs, several miles up the track from our end of the shire, the smart set were throwing parties after their parents had gone out, and at these parties what went by the vague soubriquet of *getting off* was not only permissible but compulsory. Couples were assumed to be sexually active because the assumption was trendy, and those who were left alone felt this as failure.

Even at the time, I suspected everybody hated the rituals, the ear-busting level of noise from lousy speakers, the lack of dignity upon which the whole thing was predicated. But we went, desperate to *fit in* and to see what happened when we knocked back three different kinds of alcohol. We postured, pawed strangers and said things we regretted, keeping our fingers crossed. Which was much the way we dealt with contraception.

We were not ignorant. Not completely. We saw nakedness in the cinema and knew French kissing had a lot to answer for. Most of us were aware that mass-produced chemical and barrier devices existed and that the responsible thing to do was seek them out. But we suffered from half-shame, half-fears and idiotic priorities. Condoms were *uncool*, passé and suspiciously soft (*that's a woman's problem, doll – all those mean to me is loss of sensation*) and IUDs were for grown-ups who didn't mind being studded with internal metal hooks that all too easily failed. The Pill, however, its name uttered in hushed tones with a capital P to show respect, was the Princess of Preventives. Pretty-pink and sugar-coated, it promised a girl could have her cake without *the consequences* by the simple expedient of popping one a day from a foil-sealed pack and swallowing it down. It seemed too good to be true and in some ways was, but modern boy and modern girl, Phillip and I discussed our relationship, as we understood modern people were meant to. We acknowledged our hopes as a couple and our default choice of last-minute withdrawal as frankly *not good enough* for clued-up trendsetters like us. The responsible thing to do – we'd read it in *Cosmopolitan* – was to head for a clinic which, if the scandal sheets were correct, handed out contraceptives like sweeties even to underage tearaways. We were over the age of consent, a stable unit and well intentioned. Being frank and easy with our parents was still a step too far, and though we were sure they had at least a clue, the etiquette of the place and times was to pretend the opposite. Our doctor still occupied the practice my mother had cleaned when I was three so we ruled him out and Phillip made an appointment with his. His doctor was a rock, he said, St Peter. Our case was cast-iron. He had every faith that Dr O'Flynn would be sensitive and kind.

Phillip was in the waiting room in his ATC greatcoat by the time I arrived. He'd had a go at shaving and his face was pink, with a cut under one ear. I wore school uniform: no make-up, no earrings, no nail varnish. Instinct had gone for bland. We agreed not to make an outright demand in case that was rude. We would *infer*. Inference was deferential and doctors like deferential. Obsequious and dewy-eyed seemed the safest route. Phillip went in first. After a couple of minutes, he came for me.

Inside the tiny surgery, Dr O'Flynn was writing on a piece of paper attached to a blotter. He looked like W.B. Yeats, wild and grey, with a creased handkerchief blousing out of a jacket pocket. He was cleaning the nib of a fountain pen with a tissue and didn't look up. He didn't invite me to sit.

This young man tells me you're here for advice. He kept his eyes on the tissue, expecting a blue emission some time soon. Out of eyeshot, I smiled. Very *specific* advice. He swung in his chair to hold his pen over the bin where it threw up ink. Sit. I sat. He put the pen back together and turned to look at us for the first time, the rims of his fingernails livid.

Advice on the subject of *contraception*. He lined his syllables up like soldiers on parade, an emphatic rank. Is that the case?

We're engaged, Phillip said. We want to be responsible about this.

We're not getting married any time soon, I said. I've got exams and you need to take your time. Phillip took my hand.

She means we're still saving up, he said. We're trying not to rush things but not take chances either.

And you're telling me this because?

We looked at the doctor and tried to work out what wasn't clear. Well, Phillip said, we were hoping you'd tell us how we get the Pill.

The Pill, Dr O'Flynn intoned.

Contraceptive pills, Phillip explained.

Phillip is allergic to latex, I said, and we ought to get something else.

Dr O'Flynn looked us up and looked us down. He gazed at our enmeshed fingers. He ran his eyes over my school tie, my viola case, my patent-leather boots.

Both over sixteen?

We nodded. He drew a sharp breath through his teeth, hissing. Well, he said. Well. He raised the pen and laid it delicately on his blotter, smearing each side of the nib as a final check of its readiness for use. He replaced the silver nib and put the pen safely aside then turned, settling one hand on each knee like a guard lion before a jade temple.

You do not ask advice, but I will give it anyway. He switched his gaze to me, straightened, and spoke very slowly. My advice is to *abstain*. There was a pause. If your eventual intention is marriage, you should be capable of waiting. If not, marry sooner. That thought alone might keep you on the straight and narrow. It served my generation well enough. He stood, crushing the top sheet of the blotter into a ball as he moved from the table to the door. And that is the voice of my heart and my convictions.

It was then I noticed the picture of the Pope on the wall near his plain block calendar. Noticing my noticing, he threw the blotter ball at me.

I will not collude in this business. He opened the door to a waiting room full of waiting people, his cheeks reduced to match-head red spots. My advice is to abstain.

I forgot, Phillip said as we stumbled up Dockhead Street in mild shock. I forgot. He's an old friend of the family. But I forgot about the Pope.

That we hadn't seen it coming was more than embarrassing; it was a serious setback. Abstain wasn't advice: it was judgement and I wasn't even sure he was allowed to do that. Either way, he had, and doctors, like teachers and every other keeper of keys, most probably closed ranks if you went to someone else and had another go. Abstain was the only advice we were getting. There were Family Planning Clinics, but I had no idea if they only dealt with married women or where you found one. The chemist had no leaflets and all the ads carried London phone numbers. We did what we could with the abstain thing but within a week I landed a part-time job as a singing waitress with a company putting on docile Burns Nights for Americans and our celebrations returned things to business as usual. We resorted to paper tissues, not prophylactics, kept calm and carried on.

It remains an oddity that our legitimate attempts to procure synthetic hormones to avoid pregnancy should have been subject to censure when we went to the pub illegally every weekend and nobody said boo. Under a carcinogenic fug from all manner of fags – Hamlet cigars, Slim Panatellas and Golden Virginia roll-ups – we could order anything on offer behind the gantry with no questions asked about our age. Phillip liked Guinness. I had vodka on the grounds it tasted of nothing if you put enough mixer in it. There was nothing I much *liked* to drink except tea, but permission to sit in the warmth of the pub rather than be blown along the windswept sand required regular buying of alcohol, and besides, pubs were a sanctioned part of British culture. Training yourself to drink alcohol was natural; the desire to avoid pregnancy was simply cheating. Looking the part was all it took to be served at the bar and sometimes not even that. Fifth and sixth years at school regularly went to the shoreline guest houses at lunchtime to buy pints and play darts wearing full uniform and it was all a bit laddish, chuckle-worthy fun. We didn't know what to think about our experiment in responsibility going AWOL, so we thought nothing. Sex was bad and booze was good. Tradition. *O tempora, o mores. O Caledonia.* ∎

Black Against the Sky, the Giant Mothers

Black against the sky the giant mothers
are whispering together in the moonlight –
one of which, the boniest, is mine.
She stuffs my ears with centipedes and millipedes,
she crams my little mouth with bones and tongues,
she pulls my nipples in and out and beats me
with mittens made of pigskin and blood.
We never kiss. We never even try.
We never talk. She's taught me not to talk.
The things we never talk about are private.

She's taught me not to want what I want.
She's taught me not to hope – God forbid –
not to laugh, and not to cry in pain;
not to hear the cries of pain of others,
not to seek and not to find; she's taught me
to know my place, which is complete darkness,
where things you touch are huge beyond belief
and when you walk you need to walk on tiptoe,
circumspectly, like the slow loris
hunters trap to steal their rare eyes.

Black
Clock

Aimee Bender · Tom Carson · Samuel R. Delany · Don DeLillo
Brian Evenson · Janet Fitch · Rebecca Newberger Goldstein · Maureen Howard
Shelley Jackson · Heidi Julavits · Miranda July · Jonathan Lethem · Ben Marcus
Greil Marcus · Rick Moody · Geoff Nicholson · Geoffrey O'Brien
Richard Powers · Joanna Scott · Darcey Steinke · Susan Straight
LynneTillman · David L. Ulin · Michael Ventura · William T. Vollmann
David Foster Wallace · Carlos Ruiz Zafón

───────

EDITOR Steve Erickson

subscribe online   www.blackclock.org
Published by CalArts in association with the MFA Writing Program

ALL I KNOW ABOUT GERTRUDE STEIN

Jeanette Winterson

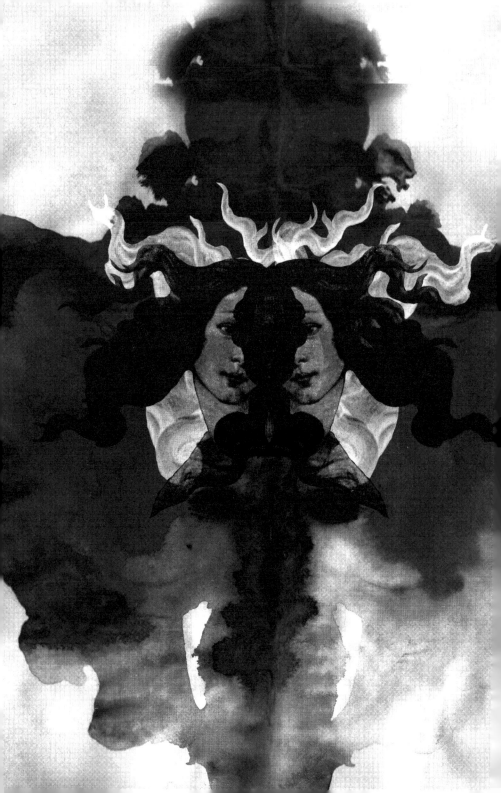

In 1907 a woman from San Francisco named Alice B. Toklas arrived in Paris. She was going to meet a fellow American living there already. She was excited because she'd heard a lot about Gertrude Stein.

In 2011 a woman from London named Louise was travelling by Eurostar to Paris. Louise was troubled. Louise was travelling alone because she was trying to understand something about love.

Louise was in a relationship; it felt like a ship, though her vessel was a small boat rowed by herself with a cabin for her lover. Her lover's ship was much bigger and carried crew and passengers. There was always a party going on. Her lover was at the centre of a busy world. Louise was her own world; self-contained, solitary, intense. She did not know how to reconcile these opposites – if opposites they were – and to make things more complicated, it was Louise who wanted the two of them to live together. Her lover said no – they were good as they were – and the solitary Louise and the sociable lover could not be in the same boat.

And so Louise was travelling alone to Paris.

I am Louise.

I took the Metro to Cité. I walked past Notre-Dame and thought of the hunchback Quasimodo swinging his misshapen body across the bell-ropes of love for Esmeralda. Quasimodo was a deaf mute. Cupid is blind. Freud called love an 'overestimation of the object'. But I would swing through the ringing world for you.

Alice Toklas had no previous experience of love.

Her mother died young – young for the mother and young for Alice – and Alice played the piano and kept house for her father and brothers. She ordered the meat, managed the budget, supervised the kitchen. And then she came to Paris and met Gertrude Stein.

Gertrude Stein's mother died young too – and you never fully recover from that – actually you never recover at all; you take it with you as an open wound – but with luck that is not the end of the story.

Gertrude had a modest but sufficient private income. She and her brother Leo had long since left the USA to set up house in Paris in the rue de Fleurus. Gertrude wrote. Leo painted. They bought modern art. They bought Matisse when no one did and they bought Picasso when no one did. Pablo and Gertrude became great friends.

But Gertrude was lonely. Gertrude was a writer. Gertrude was lonely.

I find myself returning again and again to the same familiar condition of solitariness. Is it sex that makes this happen? If it were not for sex, wouldn't we each be content with our friends, their companionship and confidences? I love my friends. I am a good friend. But with my lover I begin to feel alone.

A friend of mine can be happy without a lover; she will have an affair if she wants one, but she doesn't take the trouble to love.

I do very badly without a lover. I pine, I sigh, I sleep, I dream, I set the table for two and stare into the empty chair. I could invite a friend – sometimes I do – but that is not the point; the point is that I am always wondering where you are even when you don't exist.

Sometimes I have affairs. But though I enjoy the bed, I feel angry at the fraud; the closeness without the cost.

I know what the cost is: the more I love you, the more I feel alone.

On 23 May 1907 Gertrude Stein met Alice B. Toklas.

Gertrude: Fat, sexy, genial, powerful.

Alice: A tiny unicorn, nervous, clever, watchful, determined.

When Gertrude opened the door to the atelier of 27 rue de Fleurus, Alice tried to sit down but couldn't, because the chairs were Stein-size and Alice was Toklas-size and her feet did not reach the floor.

'The world keeps turning round and round,' said Gertrude, 'but you have to sit somewhere.'

I sat opposite you and I liked your dishevelled look; hair in your eyes and your clothes a strategic mess. We were both survivors of other shipwrecks. You looked sad. I wanted to see you again.

For a while we corresponded by email, charming each other in fonts and pixels. Did you . . . do you . . . would you like to . . . I wonder if . . .

Every day Miss Toklas sent a petit bleu *to Miss Stein to arrange a walk in the Luxembourg Gardens or a visit to a bookshop or to look at pictures.*

One day Alice was late. Gertrude was so angry. Alice picked up her gloves to leave but as she was walking across the courtyard Gertrude called out, 'It is not too late to go for a walk.'

We went walking on Hampstead Heath. We walked for two hours straight ahead going round in circles. The circles were the two compass-turns of your desire and mine. The overlap is where we kissed.

The Stein and Toklas love affair was about sex.

They went on holiday together – the dripping heat of Italy and Gertrude liking to walk in the noonday sun.

They talked about *The Taming of the Shrew* – that play by Shakespeare – the one where Petruchio breaks Kate into loving him – a strange play. Not a poster-play for feminism.

GERTRUDE: A wife hangs upon her husband – that is what Shakespeare says.

ALICE: But you have never married.

GERTRUDE: I would like a wife.

ALICE: What kind of a wife would she be?

GERTRUDE: Ardent, able, clever, present. Yes, very present.

ALICE: I am going back to San Francisco in ten days.

GERTRUDE: I have enjoyed your visits every day to the rue de Fleurus . . .

And they walked in silence up the hill into the crest of the sun and Alice began to shed her clothes – her stockings, her cherry-red corset.

Alice began to undress the past. At the top of the hill they sat down and Gertrude did not look at her.

GERTRUDE: When all is said one is wedded to bed.

It was the beginning of their love affair.

I met my lover two years ago and I fell in love. I fell like a stray star caught in the orbit of Venus. Love had me. Love held me. Love like wrist-cords. Love like a voice from a long way off. I love your voice on the phone.

Below me on the *quai* there's a skinny boy singing to his guitar: All You Need is Love. Couples holding hands throw him coins because they want to believe that it is true. They want to believe that they are true.

But the love question is harder to solve than the Grand Unified Theory of Everything.

If you were Dante you'd say they were the same thing – 'the love that moves the sun and the other stars'.

But love is in trouble.

Women used to be in charge of love – it was our whole domain, the business of our lives, to give love to make love to mend love to tend love.

Men needed women to be love so that men could do all the things you can't do without love – but no one acknowledged the secret necessity of love. Except in those dedications: To My Wife.

Now we have our own money and we can vote. We are career-women. (No such word as career-man.) We are more than the love interest. More than love. We are independent. Equal.

But . . . What happened to love?

We were confident that love would always be there, like air, like water, like summer, like sun. Love could take care of itself. We didn't notice the quiet tending of love, the small daily repairs to the fabric of love. The faithful gigantic work that kept love as regular as light.

Love is an ecosystem like any other. You can't drain it and strip-mine it, drill it and build over it and wonder where the birds and the bees have gone.

Love is where we want to live. Planet Love.

When we met, the most surprising and touching thing to me was that you always answered your phone when I called. You were not too important to be available. You are important but you recognized love as more important.

I started to believe you. I started to believe in you. Love has a religious quality to it – it depends on the unseen and it makes miracles out of itself. And there is always a sacrifice. I don't think we talk about love in real terms any more. We talk about partnership. We talk about romance. We talk about sex. We talk about divorce. I don't think we talk about love at all.

Alice Toklas never went back to San Francisco. She never saw her family again. Gertrude's brother Leo soon moved out of the rue de Fleurus and Alice moved in. They were together every day for the next forty years. Shall I write that again? *They were together every day for the next forty years* . . . And they never stopped having sex.

Gertrude Stein liked giving Alice an orgasm – she called it 'making a cow come out'. Nobody knows why – unless Alice made *moo* noises when she hit it. Gertrude said, 'I am the best cow-giver in the world.' Gertrude Stein liked repetition too – of verbs and words and orgasms.

We love the habits of love. The way you wear your hair. The way you drink your coffee. The way you turn your back on me in the mornings so that I will shift to fit myself round you. The way you open the door when you see me coming home. When I leave I look up at the window and I know you will be watching me, watching over me go.

And at the same time love needs to be new every day. The fresh damp risen-up feel of love.

Gertrude Stein said – *There is no there there* – at once refusing materiality and consolation.

I am lonely when I love because I feel the immensity of the task

– the stoking and tending of love. I feel unable, overwhelmed. I feel I can only fail. So I hide and I cling all at once. I need you near me, in my house, but I don't want you to find my hiding place. Hold me. Don't come too close.

I decided to walk to the Musée Picasso because the Picasso portrait of Gertrude Stein was on loan there from the Metropolitan Museum of Art, New York. It is a famous picture. Gertrude is massy in the frame, her head almost a kabuki mask. It doesn't look like her but it couldn't be anyone else. Picasso took ninety sittings to paint it and couldn't get the head right. Gertrude said, *'Paint it out and paint it in when I am not there.'*

Picasso did that and Gertrude was very pleased. She hung the picture over her fireplace, and during the Second World War she and Alice took it to the countryside for five years, wrapped in a sheet, in their old open-topped Ford.

Gertrude said to Picasso, *'Paint what is really there. Not what you can see, but what is really there.'*

How can I trust myself like that? To see through the screens that shield me from love and not be so afraid of what I see that I break up, break off, or settle for the diluted version?

I have done all those things before.

And when I am not doing those things I am telling myself that I am an independent woman who should not be limited by/to love.

But love has no limits. Love seems to be a continuous condition like the universe. But the universe is remote except for this planet we call home, and love means nothing unless it is real and in our hands.

Give me your hand.

There's a school party at the museum. They are not looking at Picasso; they are giggling over an iPhone. Poor kids, they're all on Facebook posting themselves at a party. They are all having sex all the time because fucking is the new frigid. Look at their Facebook faces, defiant, unhappy. The F-words. Facebook, fucking, frigid, faking it.

G ertrude Stein called the generation between the wars 'the lost generation'. We are the upgrade generation. Get a new model; phone girlfriend car. Gertrude Stein hated commas. You can see why when car phone girlfriend are the same and interchangeable. Why would I work with love when I can replace the object of love?

Men still trade in their women – nothing feminism can do about that. Now women trade in themselves – new breasts, new face, new body. What will happen to these girls giggling over their iPhones?

They are the upload generation. Neophytes in the service of the savage god of the social network.

Fear. F is for fear.

In this bleak and broken world, what chance is there for love? Love is dating sites and bytes of love. Love is a stream of body parts. But if we part, I want to know that love had time enough. It takes a long time to be close to you.

G ertrude Stein could not be rushed, although she did not like to be kept waiting. Her time was her own. She had a big white poodle called Basket and she walked herself and her poodle round Paris.

Sometimes Basket went in the car with Gertrude and Alice and Alice went into the shops – and she liked that – and Gertrude stayed in the car – and she liked that. She wrote things in her notebook. She wrote every day but only for half an hour.

'*It takes a lot of time to write for half an hour,*' said Gertrude.

She wrote unpublished for thirty years. And then, in 1934, written in six weeks, *The Autobiography of Alice B. Toklas* by Gertrude Stein became a huge best-seller. Gertrude and Alice boarded the SS *Champion* and sailed for New York. Alice got a fur coat. Gertrude got a leopard-skin cap. Their travelling suits were made by Pierre Balmain. He was just a boy in those days.

When they and their outfits arrived in New York City, the ticker tape in Times Square tweeted:

GERTRUDE STEIN HAS LANDED IN NEW YORK.

'*As if we did not know it . . .*' said Alice.

The pressmen surrounded the Algonquin Hotel. The vendors selling frankfurters and pretzels watched from across the street.

VENDOR 1: The fat one built like a boulder, that's Gertrude Stein.

VENDOR 2: The thin one cut like a chisel . . .

VENDOR 1: That's Alice B. Toklas.

The press bulbs flashed like they were movie stars.

PRESSMAN: Hey, Miss Stein, why don't you write the way you talk? (Laughter.)

GERTRUDE: Why don't you read the way I write?

Everyone is laughing. Gertrude loves fame. Fame loves Gertrude.

VENDOR 2: Where's the husbands?

VENDOR 1: They got no husbands. (He passes a frankfurter through a pretzel and nods significantly.)

VENDOR 2: (low whistle) No kidding? But ain't they American gals?

VENDOR 1: Sure, but they been living in Paris.

Living with you would be the ultimate romance. I am a romantic and that is my defence against the love-commodity. I can't buy love but I don't want to rent it either. I would like to find a way to make the days with you be ours. I would like to bring my bag and unpack it.

You say we will fail, get frustrated, fall out, fight. All the F-words.

But there is another one: forgive.

In 1946 Gertrude Stein was suddenly admitted to the American Hospital at Neuilly. She had stomach cancer.

Only a few months earlier they had come back to Paris, in

1945 – the war over at last – to find the seal of the Gestapo on their apartment. Their silver and linen had been taken and the pictures were packed up ready to be removed to German art collections – that's what happened if you were a Jew.

Alice had been so upset, but Gertrude wanted to get her portrait by Picasso hung over the fireplace again, sit down in their two armchairs either side of the fire, and have some tea.

'*The apartment is here. You are here. I am here,*' she said.

At the hospital the doctor came into the room. They administered the anaesthetic. Gertrude had been advised against an operation but she did not believe in death – at least not for her. She did not believe in the afterlife either. There was no *there there*. Everything was *here*. Gertrude Stein was present tense.

She held Alice's hand. She said to Alice, *What is the answer?* But Alice was crying and only shook her head. Gertrude laughed her big rich laugh. 'Then what is the question?'

The trolley bearing Gertrude was wheeled away. Alice walked beside her lover as though she were walking beside her whole life. Gertrude never came back.

The question is: How do we love?

It is a personal question each to each, intense, private, frightening, necessary. It is a world question too, angry, refusing, demanding, difficult.

Love is not sentimental. Love is not second best.

Women will have to take up arms for love.

Take me in your arms. This is the Here that we have. ∎

Portobello

'Paul Kingsnorth travels England, from rural communities bereft of basic services, to Soho's Chinatown, which is in danger of becoming a theme park, and finds the idea of the English village is still alive - but barely, and everywhere threatened'
Guardian

On the asset-stripping and blanding of England

Now in paperback

PEN AMERICA #13

Featuring fiction by Don DeLillo, poetry by John Ashbery,
Patti Smith and Jonathan Lethem in conversation,
& much more. Visit *pen.org/journal*

The Society of Authors

The K Blundell Trust
Grants for Authors under 40

Grants are offered to writers under the age of 40 who have already published at least one book and who require funding for important research, travel or other expenditure relating to their next book, which must contribute to the greater understanding of existing social and economic organization.

Closing dates for all applications are 30th April and 30th September 2011

Full details from www.societyofauthors.org or send sae to Paula Johnson, The Society of Authors, 84 Drayton Gardens, London SW10 9SB

The Royal Society of Literature Jerwood Awards for Non-Fiction

The Royal Society of Literature and Jerwood Charitable Foundation are again offering three joint awards – one of £10,000, and two of £5,000.

These awards are open to writers engaged on their first commissioned works of non-fiction. UK and Irish citizens and those who have been resident in the UK for three years are all eligible.

Applications must be submitted by Monday 3rd October 2011.

For entry form see www.rslit.org or email Paula Johnson for further details at paula@rslit.org

The Society of Authors

Grants for Authors

Within the Authors' Foundation, which offers grants to writers of fiction, non-fiction and poetry, the following specific awards are also available:

The Great Britain Sasakawa Grant (fiction or non-fiction about any aspect of Japanese culture or society)
Roger Deakin Awards (writing about the environment)
John Heygate Awards (travel writing)
John C Laurence Awards (promoting understanding between races)
Elizabeth Longford Grants (historical biography)
Michael Meyer Awards (theatre)
Arthur Welton Awards (poetry)

Closing dates for all applications are 30th April and 30th September 2011.
Full details from www.societyofauthors.org or send sae to:
Paula Johnson, The Society of Authors,
84 Drayton Gardens, London SW10 9SB

CONTRIBUTORS

Gillian Allnutt is the author of numerous volumes of poetry, including *How the Bicycle Shone: New and Selected Poems, Sojourner* and *Lintel.*

Laura Bell lives in Wyoming and Florida. She is the author of *Claiming Ground*, a memoir.

Urvashi Butalia is co-founder of Kali for Women, India's first feminist publisher, and is Director of its imprint Zubaan. Her works include *The Other Side of Silence: Voices from the Partition of India.*

A.S. Byatt's latest work, *Ragnarok: The End of the Gods* will be published in August by Canongate. Her books include *The Children's Book, Possession* and the quartet, *The Virgin in the Garden, Still Life, Babel Tower* and *A Whistling Woman.*

Rachel Cusk's latest works are *The Last Supper: A Summer in Italy*, a memoir, and *The Bradshaw Variations*, a novel.

Edwidge Danticat's most recent book is *Create Dangerously*, a collection of essays. She has also edited *Haiti Noir*, an anthology of stories.

Clarisse d'Arcimoles is a photographer and installation artist. Her photo series *Un-Possible Retour* was exhibited at the Saatchi Gallery as part of *Newspeak: British Art Now.*

Lydia Davis is the author, most recently, of *The Collected Stories of Lydia Davis.* Her translation from the French of Flaubert's *Madame Bovary* was published in 2010.

Louise Erdrich's 'The Ojibwe Week' is from a forthcoming revised version of her 1998 novel *The Antelope Wife.* Another novel, *The Round House,* will be published in 2012. She is the owner of Birchbark Books in Minnesota.

Janice Galloway's memoir, *All Made Up,* will be published by Granta Books in September. It is a sequel to *This Is Not About Me.*

Linda Gregerson teaches creative writing and Renaissance literature at the University of Michigan. She has written four poetry collections including *Magnetic North* and *The Woman Who Died in Her Sleep,* as well as two volumes of literary criticism.

Sadaf Halai's poetry has appeared in *Ploughshares* and various other publications. She divides her time between Toronto and Karachi.

Selima Hill's poem 'Black Against the Sky, the Giant Mothers' will be included in her next collection, *Into My Mother's Snow-Encrusted Lap*, to be published by Bloodaxe.

Maja Hrgović was born in Split, Croatia. Her first collection of short stories, *Pobjeđuje onaj kojem je manje stalo* (*He Who Cares Less, Wins*) was published last year. Her story 'Zlatka' will appear in *Best European Fiction 2012*, published by Dalkey Archive Press.

Tomislav Kuzmanović is the translator of *The Death of the Little Match Girl* (*Smrt Djevojčice sa žigicama*) by Zoran Ferić; and, with Russell Valentino, *A Castle in Romagna* (*Dvorac u Romagni*) by Igor Štiks.

Caroline Moorehead's non-fiction books include *Dancing to the Precipice*, a biography of Lucie de la Tour du Pin and *Human Cargo*, a report on refugees. 'A Train in Winter' is an extract from her book of the same title, forthcoming from Chatto & Windus in the UK and HarperCollins in the US.

Téa Obreht's first novel, *The Tiger's Wife*, was published this year.

Julie Otsuka is the author of *When the Emperor Was Divine*. 'The Children' is an extract from her forthcoming novel, *The Buddha in the Attic*, which will be published by Knopf in the US and Penguin in the UK.

Francine Prose's most recent novel is *My New American Life*. She is a Distinguished Visiting Writer at Bard College.

Taiye Selasi's debut novel, *Ghana Must Go*, will be published in 2012 by Penguin Press.

Helen Simpson is the author of five collections of short stories, the most recent of which is *In-Flight Entertainment*. Her previous books include *Four Bare Legs in a Bed and Other Stories* and *Hey Yeah Right Get a Life*.

Eudora Welty (1909–2001) published six novels, twelve collections of short stories and multiple critical essays, reviews and photography series. *What There Is to Say We Have Said: The Correspondence of Eudora Welty and William Maxwell* is forthcoming from Houghton Mifflin Harcourt.

Jeanette Winterson's novels include *The Stone Gods, Lighthousekeeping* and *Written on the Body*. A memoir, *Why Be Happy When You Could Be Normal?*, will be published in October by Jonathan Cape.

Contributing Editors
Daniel Alarcón, Diana Athill, Peter Carey, Sophie Harrison, Isabel Hilton, Blake Morrison, John Ryle, Lucretia Stewart, Edmund White.

GRANTA 115: SPRING 2011 | EVENTS

Global Feminisms: A Literary Exploration
16 May, 6.45 p.m., Asia House, 63 New Cavendish Street, London W1G 7LP
F Word contributors join Wendy Law-Yone and Moni Mohsin to discuss women's lives around the world with Deputy Editor Ellah Allfrey. Part of Asia House's Festival of Asian Literature. Please visit www.asiana.tv/tickets for tickets.

Liars' League Presents The F Word
17 May, 6.30 p.m., The Duke, 7 Roger Street, London WC1N 2PB
For this special edition of the rollicking literary salon, actors read work by Helen Simpson, Eudora Welty and Lydia Davis. Taiye Selasi will appear in person for a reading and discussion of her work in The F Word.

The Legacy: Feminism in Literature Today
18 May, 6.30 p.m., Foyles, 113–119 Charing Cross Road, London WC2H 0EB
Rachel Cusk and Taiye Selasi talk about which writers passed feminism down to them, and what the word means to them today. With readings from the issue.

Female Adventurers
19 May, 6.30 p.m., Women's Library, London Metropolitan University, 25 Old Castle Street, London E1 7NT
Caroline Moorehead and Sara Wheeler discuss the lives of daring women: the adventurer Fanny Trollope and female members of the French Resistance.

Shoreditch House Literary Salon
19 May, 7 p.m., Shoreditch House, Charles Square, London N1 6HL
Rachel Cusk joins Damian Barr's renowned literary salon. RSVP on the Shoreditch House Facebook page.

Inheritance and Motherhood: A Literary Salon
20 May, 6 p.m., The Foundling Museum, 40 Brunswick Square, London WC1N 1AZ
An evening of art, history and literature.

Guests will have a private view of the Foundling Voices exhibition followed by a discussion with the curator and with F Word contributor Caroline Moorehead. Moderated by Deputy Editor Ellah Allfrey. Cash bar. Donation to museum suggested. Limited tickets; email events@granta.com.

To Origin and Nurture
23 May, 6.45 p.m., British Library Conference Centre, 96 Euston Road, London NW1 2DB
Join poets Gillian Allnutt and Linda Gregerson for an evening of poetry and conversation. RSVP to Eccles-centre@bl.uk.

The Legacy: Feminism in Literature Today
24 May, 2 p.m., Book Expo America, Jacob K. Javits Convention Center, 655 W 34th Street, New York 10001
Julie Otsuka, Francine Prose and other *Granta* contributors talk about which writers passed feminism down to them, and what the word means to them today. For tickets, visit www.bookexpoamerica.com.

The F Word Launch Party in NYC
25 May, 6.30 p.m., Paragraph, 35 W 14th Street, New York 10011
Join Julie Otsuka and Francine Prose to celebrate the launch of the issue.

Truly Yours, Eudora Welty
10 June, 7 p.m., Wollman Hall, The New School, 66 W 11th Street, New York 10014
A discussion about Eudora Welty with writers who have been influenced by her, and a reading of her unforgettable job application letter to *The New Yorker*. Moderated by Assistant Editor Patrick Ryan.

The Granta F Word Launch with Writers' Centre Norwich
20 June, 7 p.m., Norwich Playhouse, 42–58 St George's Street, Norwich NR3 1AB
A celebration of The F Word, with Maja Hrgović and Urvashi Butalia. Please visit www.writerscentrenorwich.org.uk for more information.